SORRY ABOUT THE MESS

HELLOGREEDO

Thank you to my wife and daughter.
I'm the luckiest guy in the world.

Thanks to my viewers and supporters.
You all keep the channel going.

I should have hired an editor…

Copyright 2019 by HelloGreedo
All rights reserved. No portion of this book may be reproduced in any form without permission from the published, except as permitted by U.S. copyright law.

CHAPTERS

1. **THE ORIGIN STORY** | PAGE 1

2. **WHY STAR WARS?** | PAGE 33

3. **CLICKBAIT & SOCIAL MEDIA** | PAGE 54

4. **YOUTUBE** | PAGE 73

5. **MY TOP TEN MOVIES** | PAGE 93

6. **THE UNITED STATES NAVY** | PAGE 111

7. **VIDEO GAMES** | PAGE 138

8. **BEING A DAD** | PAGE 159

9. **SUPPORTER Q&A** | PAGE 175

10. **IN CLOSING** | PAGE 190

CHAPTER 1
THE ORIGIN STORY

I want to write a book...but what if no one likes it?
What if I don't have anything to say?
What if my viewers stop watching?
What if my family and friends laugh at the idea?
What if it gets bad reviews!?
What if?
WHAT IF!?

At some point I had to realize that I was basically George McFly. Making excuses. No confidence in my ideas. Constantly repeating, in my head, the line, "*I just don't think I can take that kind of rejection.*"

Writing this book was a happy accident. In

2016, I decided to enroll in two college classes that had a four hour break between them. I was excited! *Four hours of uninterrupted time to work on stuff! Hell yeah!* My goal was to use those four hours to write videos and work on general channel stuff. I began writing down random thoughts, opinions, and even cataloguing some of my life experiences. The idea to turn some of these writings into a book didn't come until I picked up Chris Stuckmann's book, *The Film Buff's Bucket List*.

Despite going full steam ahead with the book idea, those George McFly thoughts of self-doubt continued to creep in.

Who am I to think I can write a book?
I'm just a random YouTuber.
I'm just some random dude.
Who the hell would care about what I have to say?

Over the past three years, whenever I felt like writing a little bit in the book, I let my fingers fly. I was in no rush; I never thought I'd finish it anyway. It was just an idea, after all.

I have a lot of ideas running around in my

brain, but how many have I actually pursued? I've talked about writing and illustrating children's books for a decade. Those books don't exist. What about that Star Wars fan film I've been talking about making for five years? Nope. All I have are a few scripted pages. I even planned on making a Star Wars folk album from the perspective of a war-weary Stormtrooper. A few songs were written, but then the *E* string on my acoustic guitar snapped and I never bothered to fix it.

The vast majority of my ideas have never come to fruition. My computer is a graveyard of ideas; dozens of labeled folders with nothing in them, endlessly sitting in limbo until they are acted upon, purged, or my computer is reformatted.

I relate to George McFly. A little reticent. A little introverted. He dreams big, but doesn't know how to execute. George doesn't necessarily care what people think of him, but he cares deeply about his ideas. His ideas are sacred, and he protects them; he's afraid of his ideas being shot down. He's worried that they'll be laughed at. He just can't take that kind of rejection.

George eventually got out of his comfort

zone, and all it took was a push from a friend. Well, technically the push came from his son. Regardless, it's incredible what a pep speech and a little jolt of confidence can do for someone. You may think that your ideas are dumb, but that's just a head game you're playing with yourself. One moment can change your self-perception. One action can open your eyes to what you have the ability to accomplish. One knockout punch to Biff Tannen can change the course of history.

    I used to think that the George McFly mindset was something you grew out of. I've come to realize that age has nothing to do with it. For me, the only way to overcome that reserved way of thinking has been to throw my ideas out there, rarely look at the response, and mainly ignore the feedback without contemplating how it will be received. That being said, creativity definitely breeds creativity. Ideas take form when they are tossed out into the world. If you're hoarding your creative projects for a later date, you're not doing yourself, or the world, any good. If you have something to say, and can present it in a way that represents who you are, do it. Try not to be timid. I guarantee there are people out there who want to hear what you have to say, you just have to give them the opportunity to listen.

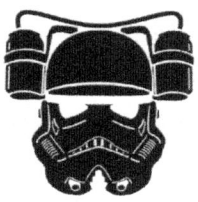

Like Superman and Batman, everything and everyone has an origin story. Mine isn't as exciting as being the last son of Krypton, or being bitten by a radioactive spider. This isn't a story about a farm boy who blew up the Death Star or a runt who was injected with super-soldier serum. The origin story of HelloGreedo is nowhere near that level of excitement. My story is probably very similar to yours. But small moments often lead us down new and intriguing paths. Hang on tight; this is going to be all over the place.

It's hard for me to remember when I first fell in love with Star Wars. The story of a restless young man, a brave princess, and a cocksure smuggler has always been a part of my life. Bad guys against good guys, a line drawn in the sand of what is right and what is wrong. Friendship, sacrifice, and working together for a common goal. The Galactic Empire trying to hold onto order through domination, and the struggle of a rebellion to break the grip of control. These plot points aren't anything revolutionary, many stories follow a similar formula, but Star Wars stood out to me.

Did I recognize the nuances when I was six years old swinging a cardboard tube making lightsaber sounds with my mouth? Of course not. Did I contemplate the philosophical intricacies of The Force when I held a tree branch like a DL-44? Nope. Star Wars was just a big sandbox that I wanted to play in. I didn't just want to be an observer; I wanted to be a participant. I wanted to walk into the Mos Eisley Cantina and tug on the bartender's shirt. I wanted to hide in the floorboards of the Millennium Falcon as Stormtroopers conducted their search. I wanted to pilot an X-Wing and destroy a technological terror. There was nothing like Star Wars. It was, and still is, tailored for my imagination.

Power of The Force was a line of Star Wars action figures released by Hasbro/Kenner in 1995. My dad showed me how to use the family's big, bulky, shoulder-mounted camcorder. I used to put it on a tripod and shoot stop-motion animation with my action figures. Move the arm a little bit, capture a frame. Move the leg a little bit, capture a frame. There were no rules. Lando Calrissian battled *Jurassic Park* dinosaurs. The *Ghostbuster's* firehouse gave everyone shelter. The radioman from the bucket of green army men called in airstrikes when the velociraptors were closing in. Batman and Superman were friends. I could let my imagination run wild in my room, creating my own little home movies.

What's crazy to me nowadays is that the big bulky camcorder has been replaced by a sleek handheld device with free and simple editing software. Everyone has one, and it's amazing! The modern democratization of technology is incredible. There are no more boundaries. No middle-men. If you want to make something, nothing is stopping you.

So many parents want to rip these devices out of their kid's hands. I get it. They can be distracting. Many mobile games remind me of Vegas slot machines, and Vegas slot machines remind me of NASA's early monkey experiments. *DING! DING! DING!* Bright lights ignite when you hit the correct button, sending a rush of dopamine to your brain. You did it! You figured out the puzzle! Here, have a tasty treat, Primate!

Moderation is key, of course. But distractions aren't always a negative. Distractions can sometimes be an indicator pointing towards what a kid is into. If a kid likes to watch a certain show, there's no harm in explaining that there are people behind the scenes who create the show.

"You mean I can make money writing stories!?"
"My job can be drawing characters for video games!?"
"I can hold a camera for a living?"

You never know when a spark could be lit. Don't automatically snatch the device out of the kid's hand. Show some interest in their interests.

I realize that I've only been a father for a blink of an eye, so I'm sure I'll change my tune when my daughter is older. If you're a parent, you probably rolled your eyes at the last paragraph. But I don't think there's anything wrong with feeding curiosity, and explaining potentials. Computers are, and have been, the future for a very long time. Then again, there are a myriad of downsides to putting a small electronic device in a kid's hand.

If you follow my YouTube Channel, you know I have a tendency to go on random tangents. That was one of them. You'll encounter plenty more random nonsense throughout the book. All sales are final. No taksies backsies. Sorry about the mess.

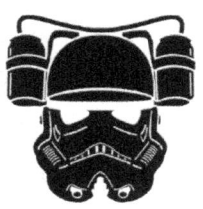

I was never sheltered as a kid. Rated R movies and parental advisory albums were never prohibited in our house. Watching Officer Alex J. Murphy be turned into a bullet sponge in *Robocop* never bothered me. John McClane saying *"Yippee-ki-yay, motherfucker"* didn't scar me for life. It all desensitized me, in a good way.

I remember having a sleepover party for my

birthday when I was in third grade. My friends and I watched *Alien*. Were we too young? Yeah, probably. One of my friends at the sleepover started feeling sick after the alien exploded out of John Hurt's chest. He puked. His mom came and picked him up. I watched *Candyman* with another one of my friends, and he puked when the bees were wallowing around in Tony Todd's mouth.

I never understood it. It's just a movie. There weren't *really* bees in his mouth. An alien didn't *really* burst out of his chest.

In 1994, I was 8 years old. I remember coming out of my bedroom, groggy, unable to sleep, and my parents were watching the newly released VHS copy of the movie *Speed*. They let me sit down and watch it with them. It's still one of my favorite action movies of all time. Looking back, I'm extremely grateful that I was never held back from seeing or hearing anything. Words are just words. Movie violence is just movie violence.

Of course, the game has majorly changed since those days. The internet has turned the ability to shield a kid from something nearly impossible. If a kid wants to see a boob, all they have to do is type 'boob' into Google. If they want to watch a movie, no parental lock can stop them. If the edited version of a song plays on the radio, they're not dumb, they know the real lyric isn't *'forget you'*. Kids are born with technology in their hands. It's getting harder and harder to be a bullshitter.

I was born in Columbus, Ohio. My family and I moved to Atlanta, Georgia when I was five years old. In Atlanta I played a lot of laser tag; Q-Zar to be exact. Wars were fought with pinecones, and the defending faction stood their ground in the backyard playhouse. My fingers hopped from button to button on the Nintendo controller, carefully leaping Mario over deadly caverns. My friends and I would buckle our rollerblades and play street hockey in the cul-de-sac. I'd go across the street to my friend's house to play fantasy board games like *Talisman* with his super nerdy dad. I played a lot of baseball, something I regret not pursuing in my high school years. I had an amazing childhood. Nothing but good memories and awesome parents.

When I was around ten years old, there was a kid on my baseball team who was an absolute shit-head. He would constantly hit people. He'd just punch everyone in the stomach and arms. It was like some tick he had, or maybe he was just a wild ass kid who couldn't be tamed ... or maybe he learned it from his home life. Who knows. Baseball practice had ended that day, and my dad and I were walking towards the car to leave. My dad asked about the kid, because he saw him punching me. I told him that he hit everyone, not just me. My dad told me what I would probably tell my own kid. He told me to hit him back. So, the next time that kid tried to punch me, I hit him back as hard as I could. After I defended myself and showed that I couldn't be pushed around, that little shit never used me as a punching bag again.

Drawing was a big part of my life at the time. Being a huge *Indiana Jones* fan I would always doodle scenes from the movies, and one time I ended up drawing a picture of *Indiana Jones* on my homework. This particular masterpiece was of Indiana swinging onto a big truck. My mom saw it and immediately told me to erase it. *Why?!! What's so bad about Indiana swinging onto a big truck, mom!?* Well, it turns out that I didn't quite understand the historic significance of a certain part of the drawing. I saw it a million times while Indiana was kicking ass, and had no idea what it truly represented. I drew a swastika. I drew a big fat stupid swastika on the side of the truck. I had to erase my Indiana Jones drawing. Fucking Nazis.

There was a guy who lived across the street from us who worked with computers. Home computing was a relatively new thing, and the internet was an exciting new frontier. He showed me *Duke Nukem 3D* when it came out, and my mind was blown. My family had a computer, but I don't remember showing much interest in it until then. When I installed *Duke Nukem 3D*, it changed my life. Video games had always been a big part of my youth prior to *Duke*, but this was something new. It felt like I was connected to the rest of the world.

Oh, and then there was 'adult mode'. To this day I don't know if my parents knew about 'adult mode'. Blood, cursing, and pixelated nudity; the three major food groups for any adolescent young boy.

Playing that game gave me a deep love for PC gaming; a love that has never gone away.

When *Diablo* was released, that love grew even stronger. *Diablo* was the first time I ever played with people from around the globe. It was the first time I linked up with my friends over a 28k modem, and slayed the beasts of Hell while wearing my *Godly Plate of the Whale*.

Don't you dare pick up the phone, mom!

We moved to Jacksonville, Florida when I was 12 years old. I played baseball until I hit high school (I was a left-handed pitcher with a submarine release. I wish I would have stuck with it.). Paintball was all the rage, and my friends and I would often play in under-construction homes. The guitar was something I picked up, which led to forming a band with some of my high school friends. I discovered *Counter Strike* and *Ultima Online*, two PC games that would consume my life for years to come.

In high school I was friends with some big pranksters, and I fit right in. We would often fill up giant super soakers, drive around the mall, and spray classmates that we recognized. Car chases would often ensue. Those were always fun nights. One of our favorite pastimes was to drive around the neighborhood, connecting to random unsecured home Wi-Fi signals with printers, and max out the printing queue with pages of porn. We were teenagers with freshly printed driver's licenses, and the night was ours.

I was never a good student. Sure, I enjoyed the subjects that I was interested in, but the other subjects were there to kill time. I loved English class, because I had an interest in writing. I loved computer art, because I was already interested in design. Other than those two subjects, I didn't show much interest. What's interesting is that I never skipped a single day of high school. I went to school every single day, and never once thought about skipping. I actually had a lot of fun. Great friends, a few fantastic teachers, and zero enemies. I got along with everyone.

There was one teacher who was the embodiment of a soul-crusher, a dream-snatcher, and an all-around ass. The kind of person who thinks they're always right. The kind of person who folk singers sing about for trampling dreams. My schedule was always filled with art classes, so I typically carried a sketch book with me throughout the day. I can remember this like yesterday, which is sad. I had my sketch pad on my desk. I wasn't touching it. The teacher looked down and said, "*Art will never get you anywhere.*" Huh? What? Are you kidding me? If she said that to me that today, as a 32 year old man, a tirade of flowery language would be launched her way. But to say that to a kid? A kid who loves art?! A kid who wanted nothing more than to be a Disney animator when he grew up?

Fu-uh-uh-uh-uck you.

It turns out that so many people who had her as a teacher had a similar experience. She was the queen of bullshit, and ruled over a kingdom of demoralized kids. She was the brightest example of someone who should not be an educator. It's funny how an experience like that can stay in your head for so many years. She taught math, and until that encounter I never had an issue with math. I wasn't good at it by any stretch of the imagination, but I could manage. After that, I had zero desire to put any effort into math. It completely turned me off to the subject. It doesn't bother me anymore on a personal level, but what does bother me is that she's still a teacher. There are still kids out there who are sitting in her classroom, and having their passions questioned.

My younger sister actually had this particular teacher, too. She's now a teacher herself; a damn good one at that. She said she's trying to repair the damage done by that asshole. Respect.

My next door neighbor, Joe, was a big Star Wars fan. When we were in 9th grade, we'd often have what we called *Star Wars Freak Nights*. I'm not sure why we called it that. It sounds kind of weird when you say it out loud. After a night of running around the neighborhood and shooting BB guns at porta potties, we'd retreat inside to watch Star Wars. *Be kind, rewind* never applied. Those VHS tapes were mine, and they always sat on my bedroom's TV stand. Our goal was to watch all three original trilogy movies in one night. Did we ever succeed? I honestly don't remember. Do you remember, Joe? Text me if you do.

The success of our late night mission wasn't important, it was about coming together over something that we both enjoyed. We found common ground in our love for Star Wars.

Space exploration and astronomy have always been the two things I'm most fascinated by. My heroes are astronauts and astronomers of all eras. The mystery of it all is what drives me to it. The feeling that stirs inside of me when I look at the Hubble Deep Field image must be what our ancestors felt when they gazed out at the vast oceans.

The famed Hubble Deep Field is an image taken by the Hubble Space Telescope. The image is of a small region of our sky, and it contains as many as 10,000 galaxies. Look it up. Seriously, if you've never seen it, Google it.

If the Hubble Deep Field doesn't stir your sense of wonder and make you question everything you've been taught, I don't know else would.

I can think of no nobler of a task than exploring for the sake of scientific progress and propelling humanity into new frontiers.

My fascination with space without a doubt stemmed from my dad. He's always been into the subject. He gave me all of his Carl Sagan books. We've seen multiple shuttle launches together. It's a constant topic of discussion.

Our circumstance in the universe never ceases to amaze me. We're on a rock spinning around a star, which is a small part of a galaxy made up of hundreds of billions of stars, in a universe made up of hundreds of billions, or trillions, of galaxies; each with hundreds of billions, or trillions, of stars. Pondering the scale and scope of what is beyond our home planet makes my brain spin.

The scale and scope is why I find people who adamantly believe, or have the default position that, we are the only *intelligent* life in the universe to be an incredibly narrow minded position.

If they're out there, why haven't we found them!? When these types of statements are uttered, I actually get excited to have the discussion that follows. Explaining the speed of light, radio communication, how massive the universe is, and how slow our methods of transmission are relative to the distances between objects. Hell, the closest neighboring star system to us is 4.22 light years away. Our galaxy, the Milky Way Galaxy, has a diameter of one-hundred thousand light-years. The closest galaxy to our galaxy, the Andromeda galaxy, is 2.5 million light-years away. The distances are inconceivable.

We've only been sending and receiving signals, or exploring space with modern technology, for as long as our grandparents are old. To have the default position that there is no intelligent life in the universe because we haven't found it, is to scoop soil with your hand, rummage through the clump of dirt, and deduce that Earth is void of life. Humanity has barely begun to peel back the curtain of the cosmos; there will no doubt be countless wonders to discover in the future.

Fast forward to 2005, the midnight premiere of *Star Wars Episode III: Revenge of the Sith*. My friends and I were packed into the car, on our way to the movie theater. Our excitement levels were through the roof! The line for the midnight showing wrapped around the movie theater, and everyone eagerly awaited the next installment of the saga.

I wore a *Don Post* Greedo mask, my dad's green work coveralls, some black rubber gloves, an orange vest that I picked up from a thrift shop, and a homemade blaster strapped to a homemade holster. My buddy dressed up as Han Solo. He also had a homemade blaster, and his entire costume was basically sewn together by his mom (she did an amazing job). We looked pretty damn good, if I do say so myself. It's amazing how a modified Nerf gun and some plumbing parts can look like a realistic blaster (we'd be arrested nowadays.).

The line started to move, and the mob of crazed Star Wars fans were let into the theater. Lightsabers waved. Wookiees roared. Everyone booed the previews. The lights dimmed.

20th Century Fox.
Cheer.
Lucasfilm.
Cheer.
A Long Time Ago In a Galaxy Far, Far Away…
A hush fell over the crowd.
STAR WARS!

The score came blaring through the speakers, and the crowd went wild. It didn't feel like we were going to see a movie. Everyone in that theater was participating in an event. A movie going experience that, as goofy as it sounds, we could tell our children about.

Star Wars was our denomination, and the movie theater was our place of worship. George

Lucas led the congregation, and John Williams wrote our hymns. Vader, Luke, and the Holy Force.

Amazement is the correct word to describe that night. At the time, I thoroughly enjoyed *Revenge of the Sith*. In hindsight, it doesn't hold a candle to any film in the original trilogy in my opinion. Regardless, I was mesmerized. The film ended in a reminiscent fashion, a foreshadowing of things to come. It showed us imagery that we knew and loved. The Death Star was being constructed. Grand Moff Tarkin was on screen! Holy hot damn shit, Darth Vader was in the Darth Vader suit! The movie wrapped everything up in a nice little bow, and told us to go watch the original trilogy.

So, that's what I did for the next ten years. I watched the original trilogy. Rarely, if ever, going back to watch the prequels. Despite my wishy-washy feelings about the prequel trilogy, they remind me of some great times. *Revenge of the Sith* holds a special place in my heart. Not because I love the movie, but because the time I spent with friends that night. That was, and still is, my favorite Star Wars moment and movie-going experience.

I graduated from high school in 2004 and then

went to college on and off for a few years. It wasn't for me at the time; I lacked ambition and drive. At the first college I attended, I majored in criminal justice, and quickly realized that didn't hold my interest. I enrolled in a different college and I decided to pursue something I had a passion for and was already somewhat familiar with; computer animation. Modeling 3D characters and texturing 3D environments was a ton of fun, but my studies fell to the waste side. I just didn't have the maturity required to finish. I slacked off way too much. I procrastinated often; making Counter Strike maps instead of working on projects for school, or just having a bunch friends over to hang out. I lived in a little apartment down in Orlando, and I had an absolute blast despite not finishing school.

I dropped out of college in 2007, and I decided to enlist in the United States Navy. That decision was one of the best I've ever made. Boot camp wasn't as hard as I thought it would be. Wake up, get yelled at. Do five-hundred jumping jacks in heavy boots and full uniform, get yelled at. Walk in a straight line, get yelled at. Make your bed. Go to chow. Do what you're told. Get yelled at. It was fun!

My Recruit Division Commanders (RDC) appointed me Starboard Watch Section Leader. That basically meant I was in charge of half of the division (about forty guys) and if anyone messed up the RDC would yell at me instead of the actual person that messed up. There's something funny about getting punished for someone else's mistake. I didn't mind it, though. Shit sometimes rolls uphill. You just have to keep pushing, and realize none of it mattered once you got into the fleet.

After boot camp, I spent the next four years attached to a LAMPS (Light Airborne Multi-Purpose System) squadron. We flew Sikorsky SH-60 Seahawk helicopters. You'll read about my Navy experience in a later chapter.

From 2010 to 2011, I was on a six month deployment to South America. That's when I heard that the Star Wars saga was being released on Blu Ray. Boy oh boy, was I excited! Whenever my ship came into port, I would hunt for fresh news about the release on the internet. Yeah, I knew the theatrical cuts weren't going to be on the discs, but I didn't really care at the time. I was getting Star Wars on Blu Ray! I had never seen a Blu Ray movie before, and I honestly don't think I had ever seen a HDTV either.

> *Wait...*
> *Does that mean I need a Blu Ray player?*
> *Oh, I need an HDTV too?*
> *Worth it!*

Yes, it was 2011, and an old flame was about to get lit with a blowtorch. I bought a Playstation 3 just to be able to watch the Star Wars Blu Rays.

We were all about to experience Star Wars in high definition! The saga was being released on September 16th. I preordered my copy from MovieStop, and drove up to the midnight release. If you want to see the most passionate Star Wars fans, go to any Star Wars event at midnight. There's something magical about Star Wars at midnight. Even at MovieStop, a little store that sold new and used movies, people were dressed up to buy a box. Families dressed up as Jedi. A grown man was even dressed up as little podracing Anakin. I loved it.

The following day, a few of my friends came over for a viewing party. The first thing that really stood out to me was C-3PO's golden shine. I had never seen something on a screen that was so clear, so bright and beautiful. The picture quality was undeniably amazing. John Williams' score pumped through my surround sound, and each explosion rattled the floorboards. We weren't just watching Star Wars again; we were experiencing Star Wars in a new way. Better technology allowed us to view something we've loved our entire life, in a more cinematic way, at home! I remember having the thought, *I guess I have to buy all my favorite movies on Blu Ray now.*

Even with the additional changes made to the movies, even with the availability of fan edits, I still prefer to watch the Blu Ray version of the original trilogy. There's a certain feeling I can't quite explain about holding an official release. Don't get me wrong, I absolutely love the fan edits, and appreciate them on a deep level. They're all projects of passion, and prime examples of the love we all have for the franchise. But having an official release in my hand, boxed up and sitting on a shelf with all of the logos, legal jargon, and artwork, still takes the cake for me. Yes, they're flawed. Yes, they have been edited, changed, and manipulated. Yes, they don't necessarily represent the versions that I grew up with. But there's something special about looking at my shelf and seeing a box that brings me back to all my favorite Star Wars memories. The way I used to meticulously organize my *Nintendo Power* magazines. The way I used to carefully place my *Teenage Mutant Ninja Turtles* action figures into plastic bins. It reminds me of the numerical system all of my *Goosebumps* had to be arranged in.

After watching *A New Hope*, I turned to my buddy and said, "*I've been thinking about making YouTube videos talking about the changes made to the movies.*" He just said, "*Do it.*" Like I said earlier, encouragement is key. A simple "*do it*" might not seem like much to the person saying it, but for the person listening it could mean everything.

Armed with a little Nikon point-and-shoot I bought on deployment, I started making the first HelloGreedo video the very next day. What did I want to say? How did I want to present my thoughts? Should I be drab and serious, or should I try to incorporate some humor into the mix? How do I edit video? What the hell is a MP4?

I knew nothing, but anything can be learned.

Audio and video were things I had never messed with, but I was able to teach myself the basics. Looking back, those first few videos are very rough. You know how you feel when you look back at some of your old Facebook posts? You kind of feel embarrassed, right? *"What the hell was I thinking? Why did I say that?"* I admit that I feel a little hint of that when I watch my first videos. You have to own them though. After all, they're yours. You made them.

The beauty of creating content on a regular basis is that you can constantly upgrade your methods, tone, speech, and thoughts. You're not stuck with a single video that defines what your channel is; the channel evolves. What you make is a direct reflection of who you are at the time, but just as your personality shifts, so does your art.

Was I a little rough on the special edition changes in the beginning? Maybe. I would definitely approach my first few videos differently if I were to make them today, but knowing that is part of the fun. It shows that you're not stuck in a rut, creating the same thing over and over again. I could have continued to be super negative like I was in the past, but that wouldn't reflect who I am today. I would feel like I was lying to everyone, and lying to myself. I'd feel like I was putting on an outrage-show rather than being upfront and honest.

I love my first videos for what they are. They struck a chord with a lot of people. They were a reflection of who I was at the time. I still harbor a lot of the feelings I had back then, but the approach would be totally different if I made those first few videos today.

What's interesting to me is that those videos are most people's favorite HelloGreedo videos. Hey, that's really neat! I appreciate the hell out of them for putting the channel on the map, and I appreciate all of you guys for pushing me to continue to make stuff.

The channel was born out of a love for something that I felt was being tinkered and toyed with too much. Yes, Han shot first. Han shot only. Greedo never fired. On the surface, it may seem like geeky nitpicking, but there's a deep moral question to be had. The moral question has nothing to do with the events in the movie; it has everything to do with the movie itself. It has to do with all art forms that fall under some method of control. It has to do with taking something that means so much to so many, and changing it to fit your modern world view. George Lucas is a different man than he was in 1977. His creative decisions of today don't necessarily reflect the creative decisions he made back then. He's a different human being.

I said that I would do my first videos differently if I was to do it all over again, but that doesn't mean I would ever want to go back and change them. People like them for what they are. I respect that. You can't run away from your past, you have to appreciate the humble beginnings and the decisions you made.

HelloGreedo started as a tiny passion project that grew into something beyond my wildest expectations. A sizable subscriber base was never something I thought about, and a certain number of views was never a goal I set out to achieve. I just had something to say, and I said it.

So, with all that being said, go out and make your thing. There's no better time than right now. Seriously, put this book down and start writing your screenplay. Text your buddy and tell him you want to finally start that podcast. Turn those doodles into a graphic novel. Love cooking? Then change your major to culinary studies. Hey, your garage looks pretty empty without that screen press. The world can always use another wedding photographer. The best time to start hiking northbound on the Appalachian Trail is March (you might want to double check that). Herbs are pretty easy to grow. Yes, that phone app IS a great idea. Oh man, a food truck? You're making me hungry! Your YouTube Channel isn't going to start itself! You already have a guitar; you just have to hit record!

The time we're living in is incredible. Likeminded people from around the globe can find their niche. Your little idea can blossom, gather a following, and even inspire others to pursue their own little idea. Fast forward to the end of your movie, and skip the indifferent George McFly phase.

Stop saying, *"I don't know how"*.
Start saying, *"I don't know how, yet."*

Do it.

CHAPTER 2
WHY STAR WARS?

There's no easy way to answer that question. *Why Star Wars? WHY ANYTHING!?* Why do we love the things we love, and why do those things stick with us for so many years?

One of my friends loves professional wrestling. Why? He probably couldn't even explain why he loves it. It's not for me, but I get it. I get it that he gets it. Different strokes for different folks, and all that jazz. Some people want pulp in their orange juice, and some don't want those floating boogers. Some people like hair metal, and some people like rhythm and blues. Some people are into Apple products, and some people prefer real computers *(Ha!)*. Some people like to watch golf on TV, and some people enjoy the highly entertaining hobby of watching paint dry *(Ha, again!)*. Some people like Star Wars, and some people like the prequels *(I'm on a roll!)*. I'm just kidding, folks. We all love different aspects of Star Wars more than others and that's what makes it fun.

The point that I'm trying to make is that everyone's tastes are different. Putting someone down for what they're into is pretty dopey. It sure seems like a waste of time, effort, and energy. By the same token, if you can't take a joke about the thing that you love, you might want to let your grip weaken a little bit. You're holding on too tight. You have to be able to laugh at yourself and the goofy things you're into. Don't take yourself too serious. You'll get all wound up like a rubber band and snap at the first tug of tension.

So, why Star Wars? Well, I guess the short answer is that it's relatable. Sure, at first glance it doesn't seem very relatable. What's relatable about strange creatures populating a strange bar, on a strange planet, in a strange galaxy? How can you find any connection to a masked man with a red glowing stick and a tall hairy dog with a belt across its chest? The connection we have to it doesn't necessarily come in the form of objects or visuals; it comes in the form of storytelling. What young person can't relate to Luke Skywalker? He embodies the desire we all have to explore, experience, and chart our own path. Luke has responsibilities, but those responsibilities are put on him externally. He's not interested in those responsibilities. He longs for something greater, and feels a calling for something more.

The death of Uncle Owen and Aunt Beru was the catalyst that forced Luke to make a decision. Was he going to stay home and plow the harvest or create a new reality for himself? We all have an Uncle Owen and Aunt Beru moment in our lives. They might not be as dramatic as finding the charred bones of your relatives lying in the Tatooine sand, but every small moment leads to something new. Every decision carves a new wrinkle in the fabric of your life. That's what *A New Hope* means to me. It highlights the determination we all have within ourselves to reach for new heights and establish who you will become.

Oh, and it's fun. Pretty simple. It's just fun. Giant spaceships, daring pilots, menacing bad guys, fleshed out heroes, dogfights, lasers, glowing swords, mysticism, and great characters. I could talk all day about my personal thoughts on the philosophical and political undertones, but Star Wars is nothing without the fun factor. That's what it's all about. **Fun**. An exciting story is the vessel that caries the doctrine, and wisdom, of Star Wars. Without the fun you'd be left with something sluggish. Without the excitement you'd be left with a film that feels tedious.

A New Hope is my favorite Star Wars movie. The story of its making is incredibly inspiring. George Lucas held his ground, and made the film he wanted to make in the face of opposition. He fought against the empire, led a rebellion of young artists, and made his vision come to life. He was Luke Skywalker taking hold of the situation; determined to persevere. He accepted help from friends, included people he saw had talent, and took advice where advice was needed. Lucas and his team created the blockbuster. They invented new ways of visualizing a story on the big screen. It's very similar to today's entrepreneurs out in Silicon Valley. Young people with a vision, a deep seated drive, and an unquestionable passion can change the world. George Lucas changed the way movies are made, in every respect.

One of the biggest things that turned me onto Star Wars was the setting. Instead of the sleek and shiny environments of science fiction films at the time, Star Wars took a different approach. It gave us a lived in universe full of dirt and grime. A backdrop of corroded buildings and rusted out land speeders. A world where the elements could not be fully tamed and adaptation was paramount.

Moisture vaporators? Hell yeah, moisture vaporators. What an awesome example of attention to detail! The minutiae is what makes the universe feel alive. Little snippets of dialogue that may seem like throwaway lines at the time, can often breathe life into an unfamiliar location. They can also raise an audience's curiosity, wanting them to know more about this new exciting world.

The visual style of Star Wars is so iconic. It is instantly recognizable. Ralph McQuarrie, wherever you are, thank you.

If we're talking about visuals, we also have to talk about the sound. I can't think of another franchise that has more iconic sound effects than Star Wars. Even a mouse droid, which barely appears on screen, emits a distinct sound that we all immediately remember. Everything has a unique sound setting itself apart from everything else, and at the same time it all meshes so well with one another. Nothing seems out of place. It's all unique, but it all sounds like Star Wars.

It's funny how I can close my eyes and hear certain sounds. Small sounds. Sounds that don't really matter in the grand scheme of the films, but after so many viewings, I can hear them instantly without hesitation. Right now I'm thinking of the little droid detector that pulsates in the Mos Eisley Cantina when C-3PO walks by it. I can hear that crystal clear in my head. Why? Who knows. Maybe the reason I have a horrible memory is because all of this useless knowledge is taking up too much room on my brain's hard drive. Oh well! I love it! Ben Burtt, your work has fried my circuitry.

Smelling a memorable smell in the air and hearing a memorable sound from *Star Wars* seems to punch the same nostalgia receptors in my brain. It's like when you play a song you used to love from your youth, and you can remember all of the lyrics. *How the hell do I remember that!?* You tuck away impactful memories in a brain-folder, and occasionally open it up to get hit with some nostalgia. Singing every single lyric to *Cute Without The E*, and being able to recite the odds of successfully navigating an asteroid field (approximately 3,720 to 1), come from the same place.

The merchandising of Star Wars was a huge part of the infatuation, as well. I didn't have to sit down and put in a movie to keep my mind on it, I could carry the movie with me in the form of action figures. I could wear Han Solo on my shirt! I could have a Star Wars notebook, with a Star Wars pencil, and a Star Wars ruler! It was, and still is, everywhere. If I have to choose between a plain cereal box or a cereal box with Darth Vader on it, Vader wins every time. It's weird! Maybe it's some leftover caveman DNA that makes us want to hoard objects that we deem important, and store them away for no other reason than to have them sit on a shelf. *That's my stuff! Look at that stuff! I have stuff!*

Nowadays, I don't have a desire to buy action figures or anything like that. I haven't had that itch for a very long time. I'm not sure when the switch flipped. I used to want to grab every autograph I could, collect figures, and buy every Star Wars t-shirt I saw. Now, I have no desire for any of that. My new outlook doesn't just apply to Star Wars; simplifying my living space has become an everyday pursuit. I've tried to de-clutter in general. How much shit do I really need? The only things I collect now are coffee mugs, shot glasses, pint glasses, and t-shirts from places I've been. Things with a physical memory attached.

Like I said earlier, I can't explain why all of this Star Wars stuff means so much to me. Does it really need an explanation, though? There's a weird vibe out in the universe that pulls us towards things that we love. Call it The Force. Call it what you will. I can't explain it, but there seemed to be a natural pull on me in the direction of not only Star Wars, but movies as a whole. I love the art form. Seeing how they are made, and watching passionate people pour their heart and soul into a project, gives me an inexplicable feeling. I love Star Wars, but I love movies even more. Star Wars just happens to be my favorite movie.

I've never really gotten into the expanded universe or the countless branching stories. I've read a few books, used to have a small stack of comics that I gave away, but I don't have much of a desire to dive into it all. I have read a few modern canon books, and those have been fantastic.

Star Wars, to me, belongs on a big screen with blaring speakers and a bucket of popcorn. Does that position make me a bad Star Wars fan? Some people think it does. Obviously, I don't agree with those people. There's plenty of Star Wars to go around. You can pick and choose what appeals to you, or just embrace everything. I would never tell someone that they're not a *real* Star Wars fan if they don't like what I like. We have enough nonsensical division and tribalism in the real world, I'd rather not include it in my fandom.

Within the past year, I've been going through *The Clone Wars* TV show for the first time, and I absolutely love it. It's given me an entirely new perspective on what Star Wars is and means to so many people. Admittedly, my personal Star Wars universe has always been small; three movies, a handful of characters, the Galactic Empire, and some kickass practical effects. But watching *The Clone Wars* has completely changed that point of view. I appreciate the lore that it has added to the franchise. The show enriches characters, and gives motivations. It has really broadened my view of what Star Wars is. Do I like it as much as the original trilogy? Of course not. Do I still uncontrollably differentiate the original trilogy and *The Clone Wars* into two completely and sometimes unrelated categories of Star Wars in my brain? Yes. I can't help it.

Diving into the show this late has been like opening up a time capsule that everyone already knows the contents of. But I like doing it this way. It's fun to start a show when it's already off the air, but as we know, *The Clone Wars* is coming back. I can't wait.

The Clone Wars has given me a new appreciation for the prequels. Not necessarily the films themselves, but more appreciation for that portion of the Star Wars timeline. I now understand why people love certain characters that I felt fell flat in the films. They are far more fleshed out in the show.

Felt fell flat in the films. Felt fell flat in the films. Felt fell flat in the films. That's a tongue twister.

With the birth of my daughter I decided to buy a Kindle. That's probably the best purchase I've made in the past few years. I've been reading nonstop. One of the first books I read was *Last Shot*. The book was great! It's the first Star Wars book I've read in probably twenty years. Needless to say, I have a huge itch to start reading all of the new canon books.

While Star Wars will always belong on a giant ass screen with a giant ass bucket of popcorn, reading these adventures set in the Star Wars universe has been an imaginative experience. One that I'm sad to say I've missed out on for decades. But hey, it's never too late to dive in, and I'm glad I finally did. Reading these tales has given me another reason to love Star Wars. Broadening my originally narrow view of what the franchise was. I haven't been this excited to read since I was in elementary school, at a book fair, picking up the latest *Goosebumps*.

Different values can be learned from different Star Wars characters. Han Solo started out extremely selfish. His motivations were shallow and narcissistic. He only desired money, reward, and recognition. Han's nature was questioned by the audience from the beginning. Can we trust him? Will he betray Luke and Obi-Wan en route to Alderaan? Who is this guy hanging out in the hive of scum and villainy? Now, everyone knows Han is a smuggler with a heart of gold. But before Star Wars was a part of the zeitgeist, these were real questions. Han's character arc is one of my favorites. He finds friendship, shifts his morality, finds value in a cause greater than himself, and saves the day in the end. Hero Han!

When it comes to lessons, Yoda takes the cake. Yoda is the very definition of wisdom. Basically everything that comes out of his wrinkled lips is profound and worthy of exploration.

The quote that I found the most impactful in my own life, and something I've always tried to follow, is *"All his life has he looked away ... to the future, to the horizon. Never his mind on where he was. Hmm? What he was doing."* Yoda's lesson here is one of being in the moment, and not daydreaming about where you could be or what else you could be doing. If there's a task in front of you, knock it out, get it done, and then move forward. One step at a time; give your undivided attention to what is in the immediate.

Another one of my favorite Yoda lessons is *"Always with you what cannot be done"*. Luke constantly doubted himself, and questioned his own abilities. Before even attempting a task, he put limitations on himself; saw himself failing what he set out to accomplish. This is an incredibly self-defeating mindset to have. *I don't know how. I can't do that.* You haven't even tried, Luke! Don't fall into the trap of negativity and timidity!

Despite all the psychobabble and overanalyzing that people do with the saga (me included), it all boils down to the movies impacting people, being relatable, and being fun. What I find fascinating is how different everyone's Star Wars is. When some people think of Star Wars, they think of the original trilogy. This is the case for me, and I would suspect much of my generation. When other folks think of Star Wars, they think of the prequels. And I'd be willing to bet that when this younger generation grows up, they'll think of the sequel trilogy when they think of Star Wars.

It's a generational thing. Every generation seems to shit on the next generation's Star Wars, and when the younger generation grows up, they end up defending their generation's Star Wars. Obviously, this pattern isn't exclusive to Star Wars. The generational-divide applies to all art forms and movements of the time. Older generations have always bitched and moaned about younger generations. It's dumb. It's always been dumb.

There are a ton of people talking about how Star Wars isn't special anymore, and that modern Star Wars sucks. That's what people said when the prequels were released. Now the prequel generation is old enough to defend their Star Wars movies. Just wait for the kids nowadays to grow up and have a voice.

Star Wars isn't special anymore? Oh. Okay. Maybe it's not special to you, but it's sure as shit special to every kid I know.

The best stuff came out when I was a kid! My stuff is better! Convenient!

That being said, I really hate when I hear someone doesn't like new Star Wars. I've been there. A lot of people of my generation and older have been there. It sucks to not have the franchise that you love impact you the way it once did. Trust me, I get it. But hey, those sharp edges eventually smooth out.

I have to admit that seeing prequel fans shit all over the new sequel movies is strange to me. I think the new movies are fun. They feel like the original trilogy. *Faster and more intense*. There's a lot more to it than just that, but yeah, I've been generally happy with them. It's also strange because for like a decade the Star Wars prequels were a subject of disappointment. I spent many nights on forums in the early 2000s sifting through rage-filled posts. It feels strange because the cycle is repeating itself, and I find myself puzzled by this new wave of disappointment.

Obviously, there are things to complain about and holes to poke in all Star Wars movies. But I look at many of the complaints lodged against the sequel trilogy, and I think about the exact same things that happened in previous movies that get overlooked by those complaining. I then wonder to myself, *do we all wear blinders to the Star Wars that we grew up with? Are we incapable of seeing faults in the movies that we loved as impressionable kids?* Maybe. I've certainly been guilty of this.

I started typing this chapter two years before my daughter was born. The question "*Why Star Wars?*" now has a much different answer.

I can't tell you how excited I am to introduce my daughter to the saga. I have fond memories of watching the original trilogy with my sister and friends. It's been a constant thread in the fabric of my life, and to bring my daughter into that thread is something that will put a big smile on my face. To experience Star Wars through the eyes of a child again will be incredible.

With that being said, my daughter **does not**

have to like Star Wars. She **does not** have to like what I like. I will not be crushed or disappointed if she finds zero interest in the saga.

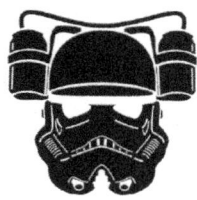

I think it's amazing that something from 1977 is as relevant today, if not more so, than ever before in its existence. There are very few things that survive the ebb and flow of culture for that long.

What's equally amazing to me is how the franchise is able to stay inventive and creative. As divisive as *The Last Jedi* is, I appreciate it for what it brought to the saga. It felt new and fresh, and is perhaps the most thought provoking Star Wars film to date. Don't mistake the term *divisive* as a synonym for *bad*. I find the fact that a Star Wars film is able to stir up so many emotions and opinions extremely exciting! If the internet, in its capacity today, was around in 1999, I'm sure the fandom would be having very similar discussions.

I really enjoy *The Last Jedi*. The more I think about it, the more it slowly creeps higher and higher on my list of favorite *Star Wars* movies. That being said, I do have a complicated relationship with it. Some of my favorite moments in the entire saga can be found in the movie, and some of my least favorite moments can be found in there as well. Overall, I think it's a solid addition to the franchise that breathes a little fresh air into what could have easily become a stagnant, predictable, and boring path. In the future, I truly believe it will be remembered as one of the better entries in the saga.

It seems as though every Star Wars fan has something they don't like in the saga, or something they want to fight for. People defend the prequels tooth and claw. Some silly gooses want to see the Disney-era films decanonized. People scream about wanting certain characters to be added to a video game. Some people make petitions for the EU to be brought back. There are a lot of passionate fans out there. Of course, it's important to be measured.

For me, there's really one thing that I adamantly fight for; the original cuts of the films being released in HD for modern viewing. It's about preserving film history, it's not about *Who Shot First.* It's about preserving the integrity of the original films. That's it. It's less geeky nitpicking, and more *it belongs in a museum.*

One of my favorite aspects of being a Star Wars fan is the anticipation. The buildup leading into *The Force Awakens* was incredibly fun. A few years of waiting patiently, reading articles, making videos, and engaging with the community. It was amazing. Sadly, I don't think we'll ever have that again. When movies are being released so frequently, the exciting slow incline to the top of the roller coaster isn't nearly as high and exciting. *Oh, another one is coming out? Didn't one just come out?* Is something I hear from family and friends quite often.

I think the one thing I'll really miss in this new hyper-Star Wars Disney age, is the anticipation. The buildup was sometimes more exciting than actually watching the damn movie. The years and months leading into a new Star Wars movie felt a lot like the night before you and your family went to Disney World. You've been waiting. Your tickets have been bought. The day has finally arrived.

The thing is, we're not really sure what

Disney's plans are. Someone in the future could be reading this right now, and laughing at me. We're not even done with the sequel trilogy yet. Disney might take a little break after Episode 9, at least from the big screen, to recalibrate. The sequel trilogy films are coming out two years apart, which I think is a good timeframe.

Is oversaturation even a thing? It is for me. There's no doubt my hype-level has died down since 2015. There's nothing wrong with that, it's natural and expected. When you have a lot of a thing, and are promised more of a thing, I think it's completely natural to not be as excited about the thing. But that's just me. All you have to do is look at Marvel movies to gauge the rest of the population. People flock to those flicks like they've never seen a superhero movie before. So, maybe I'm just being cynical. Maybe I just have to get used to the way things are.

Why Star Wars? Why anything? We love what we love. The things that bring us joy often go back to our earliest memories. Our childhood obsessions tend to hold a special place in our hearts. I think that's what all of this boils down to. We watched the movies as kids, they showed us a sandbox with endless possibilities and adventure, and now we want to pass those tales down to the next generation like stories around a campfire.

Star Wars, and movies in general, are modern mythology. Stories told, often with morals or messages, full of larger than life characters who overcome impossible odds. Star Wars teaches us about friendship, bravery, fairness, good, evil, freedom, oppression, connection, and so much more. It's mythology for a modern world.

CHAPTER 3
CLICKBAIT & SOCIAL MEDIA

There's a strange thing happening online where substance is being replaced by nonsense; outrage, tabloid sensationalism, and fake *leaked* movie scripts. Platforms that were supposed to give independent creators a voice, have become breeding grounds for the most clickbaity clickbait you can imagine. But that's not what I find strange. I suppose those cracks in the system were going to inevitably be exploited. What's strange to me is how well it thrives. What's strange to me is how people continuously go back for more. Are these viewers seeing something that I'm not?

When I see a YouTube video titled *STAR WARS EPISODE 9 PLOT LEAK!!!!!* I automatically assume it's bullshit. If I'm up for a dose of cringe and a dash of embarrassment, I'll click one. These masterpieces never say anything of substance. They barely present the advertised "plot leaks". The creator usually just talks about their own theories, and never presents anything concrete. The term "leak" seems to be used to get people to click the video; a classic bait and switch.

With the thousands of videos that fall under this category plaguing YouTube, you'd think that people would start to get wise. You'd think that the popularity of these revenue-hungry bullshit-factories would slowly start to dwindle. Nope! The free market of ideas is supposed to weed out the nonsense, but it sure as hell isn't doing that.

I play the YouTube game. I know how the revenue works. I know what you goobers are doing.

It's an easy fog to see through if you've been a creator on the site for a little while. So, instead of well thought out points inside of a creative presentation, YouTube is slowly but surely becoming the perfect swamp for mosquitos to lay their eggs. A mosquito breeds fast. They attach themselves to the host. They extract blood. They spread disease. YouTube, whether willingly or not, has allowed for the most inane content to become the front page of its platform. A hive of mosquitos looking to plunge their digital proboscis into the nearest ad revenue vein.

This virtual malaria isn't unique to YouTube, though. The entire world of online journalism has turned into a hive of scum and villainy. Want to make a decent amount of money? Buy a domain for a few bucks, toss up a legitimate looking website, and let your fingers fly as you type nonsense. Once you're done creating your work of fiction, post it on Facebook! There's no reason to push the content yourself; Just let Joe and Jane click *share*! Don't forget to have a minimum of fifteen ads on your article, though. Or maybe toss up a slideshow! You sure wouldn't want those clicks to go to waste!

A new industry was born. No substance. Nothing of value. Just some word salad and big juicy headlines.

I truly think all of this is a phase. At least I hope so. This is the first time in human history that the world's wealth of knowledge is at everyone's fingertips. There's going to be a few bumps and bruises along the way. The internet is a newly discovered ocean, and we have to learn how to navigate its waters. Despite how puzzling I find all of this, I have faith in the generation after mine.

One of the dumbest things people do is talk down to younger generations. I know it's been going on since the dawn of time; that doesn't make it any less dumb. I have so much faith in the generation after mine. They will be, or have been, born into a world of instant global communication. People don't have enemies. Nations have enemies. An individual can Skype with someone on the other side of the world, and find common ground. Classrooms have video conferences with students from other nations. We can read about the state of the world, learn about different cultures, and empathize with people from all walks of life. The idea of *us and them* is (very) slowly being eradicated, at least I hope so. I'd like to think that tribalism doesn't stand a chance in a world with the internet. As optimistic as I may seem, I find myself doubting that hope every day.

Thanks to my YouTube channel, I have talked to people from all around the globe. We might not have much in common. Our views of the world may vastly differ. But we find common ground in our love for Star Wars. We find value in the same piece of art. We share in thanks that George Lucas gave us his vision. The cultural boundaries that may stand in our way are instantly erased when I hear about someone watching a bootleg copy of Star Wars in a nation where it's restricted from being shown (fight the power). Those little similarities are the first step to dialogue and understanding. When culture is spread, we find friends. The spreading of culture is the most powerful currency and the most effective *weapon*. It has been my experience that differences are overlooked when even the smallest common ground is found.

So, when people talk shit about *Millennials* or younger generations, I can't help but roll my eyes. Older generations always find a way to criticize younger generation, never realizing that the generation before them did the same thing. It's a really stupid cycle. The news article always talks about teenagers being addicted to their phones, and while that is most certainly true, parents are equally as addicted. Maybe it will never go away. Maybe it's a reaction to losing control, and feeling like you don't have a place in a world that's moving on a forward trajectory. You were just as silly as the younger generation when you were their age, and if you weren't, how boring. If you don't think you were, you're lying to yourself. I hope I never fall into that mindset.

Speaking of millennials; it's harder for me to think of friends who don't have their own business, freelance gig, or side-project than it is to think of my friends who do. I have friends who build tables, and sell them online. I have friends who make candles, and sell them on Etsy and at local markets. I have friends who make t-shirts. I have friends who make enamel pins. I have friends who make video stock footage. I have friends who make phone apps. I have friends who make websites. Almost everyone around me is making money on the side doing something creative that they love to do. So, when I hear people talk about how lazy the millennial generation is, I am completely dumbfounded. Lazy? Bullshit. Of course some are lazy, because in general, some people are lazy. The world is different. Everyone has the opportunity to be their own boss now. Just because you don't understand how it works doesn't mean that it's lazy. The entrepreneurial candle is burning brighter than ever.

Okay, rant over. Sorry about that. There's a reason I titled this book *Sorry About The Mess*. It's messy. Where was I?

Just because I have criticism about YouTube doesn't mean I don't love it. I do. I love the hell out of it. Yeah, it has problems, but those problems will be worked out. I just feel obligated to voice my opinion on its current state. If you're thinking of starting a YouTube channel, do it. We need you.

One of my favorite things to do is search for newly created Star Wars channels, and tell them to keep up the good work. It's important to encourage new creators, because there's a lot of negativity out there. It's easy to get discouraged when you first dip your toe in the water. Seeing a positive comment that encourages you to keep making stuff is huge! If there's one thing that YouTube needs more of, it's positivity. You have the power to make someone feel like a million bucks!

YouTube has given a voice to the voiceless. It's lit the fire of controversy, it's made us laugh, it's been a vessel of information, and it's emboldened both snarky assholes and the level headed. There's no other platform like it.

Which brings me to my channel. Man, the way you guys conduct yourselves in the comment section absolutely blows me away. There's a real sense of *to each their own* going on in the comment section of HelloGreedo videos. I constantly see stuff like, "*This is just my opinion, but...*" or "*Hey, I understand where you're coming from, but...*" I love seeing that kind of stuff! There's rarely any malice or hate, and if there is malice or hate it's usually from newcomers who don't know the vibe of the channel. We all have our own opinions, but that doesn't mean you have to be a shithead if someone disagrees with you. Thanks for being awesome.

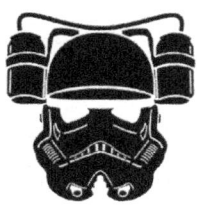

When social media started to gain traction and become popular, I dove right in. It was fun; a little way to keep in touch with friends as everyone moved away and went down separate paths. What started out as a relatively innocent addition to the internet has become something I've tried to shy away from in the past few years.

Social media has become too intrusive and cumbersome. It has become too powerful in our day-to-day lives, if one chooses to allow it. Social media almost seems designed, perhaps unintentionally by those developing the platforms, to further factional-splintering and in-fighting among populations. When the internet became accessible to all, it was seen as a promising start to spreading empathy and compassion throughout the whole of humanity. People could talk to one another; understand arguments, opinions, and hear interesting new ideas. I do not believe that to be the majority truth any longer. Perhaps it was never destined to be true.

It is far too easy to fall into e-tribes as we navigate the internet; cultivating an online experience to only hear and see things that one wants to hear and see, while blanket-demonizing those who even slightly disagree without ever actually hearing the rationale behind their opinions. A technology that promised to bring the world together seems to fracture it even further.

The amount of fake nonsense that is spread on social media is astonishing. Once again, as I said earlier, I have faith in generations born into this technology. Studies have shown that older generations have a disproportionally difficult time differentiating fact from fiction, or fake articles from true researched journalistic pieces, on the internet. The old phrase *don't believe everything you read* seems to go in one ear and out the other for some. It's disheartening. I've seen numerous people on my personal Facebook page share countless blatantly false images, articles, or memes that with no more than ten seconds of a Google search would be shown to be fake. Again, I can't stress enough how hopeful I am of future generations. They have been born into a cyberspace full of digital landmines that they will have to navigate and disarm. They will long be cleaning up after our mess.

I believe that we all have a duty to fact check and be informed without bias. We are all equipped with a bullshit detector, and a bullshit detector is a muscle that gains strength with use. There's a lot of nonsense floating out in the void, and sadly it often gets soaked up like a dry sponge. Anyone can watch a conspiracy theory video, not everyone takes the time to look into the legitimacy of its claims, or the vast library of knowledge to debunk such claims.

As Private Jackson told Corporal Upham, *"Careful you don't step in the bullshit."*

Social media has its benefits, of course. As for personal use, it's a great way to keep in touch with friends and family. As for businesses, especially small businesses, it can be a cheap and easy way to get your products and services into the marketplace. Facebook, for instance, allows businesses to create custom pages, free of charge, which are often more useful than a company's website. Twitter allows businesses to directly interact with consumers, and gauge customer interest in real-time. Businesses that use Instagram are able to capture our visual interests, and directly show products without much clutter. A company can operate, in many ways, like an individual; presenting itself almost like a friend, which usually comes off as weird to me.

Is all of that good? It's hard to say. We are witnessing the birth of direct advertising on a level that has never been experienced before. And in return for advertisements, products, and entertainment tailored to our interests, we sell a little bit of our privacy.

All of these digital systems seem to be algorithmically feeding us exactly what we want to hear and see. Therefore, we are not solely responsible for our tribalism, the artificial intelligence built into these systems are responsible as well; perhaps more so. The controls that have been placed within these systems are seemingly out of our control. The more I think about it, the more it creeps me out.

The fear of artificial intelligence that stems from science-fiction robots is not what should raise our concern; the artificial intelligence that is already here, that is invisible and working behind the scenes as we navigate the internet, warrants public suspicion.

Being in this YouTube game for eight years has also shown me how one's biases are strengthened by these algorithms. When all someone sees and hears are opinions that they already agree with because the mother ship is feeding them similar opinions, it creates an illusion of agreement. *All I see on my recommended feed are videos against X, therefor everyone must be against X!* The concept of a general consensus is harder to define, because everyone is looking through a different set of goggles. We're all being fed content that is designed to keep us nodding our heads in agreement and gluing our eyeballs to what is most likely to keep us clicking ahead. What you perceive as consensus might not be true consensus; it might just be consensus relative to what you are being fed. Weird stuff.

It's also incredibly easy to grab attention using outrage and anger, or make-believe outrage and anger. *If it bleeds it leads.* A negative non-story or headline dripping with editorialized conjecture often performs way better than something positive, or a well thought out long-form researched article void of any editorial punch, or even something with a less salacious headline. People like to roll their eyes at goofy shit that makes them mad, and it's pretty easy to spin that eye-rolling-anger into clicks; especially when one doesn't care about accuracy.

Who gives a shit if I'm accurate? I can just mention I was wrong in my next video, or write a retraction to my article that no one will read, or just never mention I was wrong and then claim others don't have integrity! GET! THOSE! CLICKS! GET! THAT! REVENUE!

When it becomes easy to predict everything that comes out of the mouth of a person or an organization on a certain topic, it becomes parody, and it's the kind of boring ass pigeonholed-thinking I try to avoid listening to or reading. When people speak in labels, acronyms, or language meant to divide and reduce the *other* into easily dismissible subcategories, I have zero desire to open an ear to that shit-thinking.

There's money in feigning outrage and fanning the flame of hyperbolic rage-bait; it's a business model. When I see websites, authors, or even video creators mulching over the same shit day in and day out, creating nothing new or interesting, I basically see them as being the internet's version of mundane divisive talk radio; a lot of conjecture, a lot of make-em-up stories, and a whole lot of believing anything and everything you read or hear without considering for one second the source it came from and its batting average.

I understand why so many creators or journalists end up covering the same thing over and over again; if they deviate from the formula even slightly, their numbers go down. Let's face it, modern journalism and monetizable discourse lives and breathes by the creativity-killing holy algorithm. Plenty of people and organizations have made careers LARPing offended and outraged over the most inane and innocuous shit, or twisting stories to fit a narrative that benefits an individual or organization despite the spin being completely out of context.

I just realized that you guys are probably filtering everything I just typed through a Star Wars lens. The funny thing is, I wasn't talking about Star Wars coverage here. It'll get taken that way, of course. I get it. Star Wars channel. Stormtrooper on the cover. No worries. It makes sense. It certainly does apply to Star Wars coverage if you choose to look at it through that lens. It wasn't my intention to make it about Star Wars coverage, because it's a problem that pokes its finger into all topics.

Anger sells. Negativity sells. Even if that anger boils up from something so incredibly harmless that you have a hard time believing anyone could be mad, people believe the anger and eat it up.

There's no money in writing middle-of-the-road stories or making middle-of-the-road videos, the money is in picking a side. There's no money in showing the humanity of those who disagree with you, you have to turn them into the *other* and make them a monster hell-bent on destroying your nation, your world, or your movie franchise! *The sky is fucking falling! Don't forget to like and subscribe so we can fight the hell beasts trying to destroy our cartoons and country!*

When it comes to social media, I've personally been trying to avoid it, or at least majorly restrict my time on it. I've found social media to be a major time-suck. It is way too easy, and tempting, to endlessly play thumb war with your phone's screen. Like I said, it's a time-suck; one that often stifles productivity. I'm on a personal crusade to manage my time more effectively than I have in the past.

When I see people sparring all day on Twitter, I find myself completely baffled. I do not understand the impulse to constantly have to say something to everyone or everything that you perceive as even slightly stepping on your toes. Oh, someone was an asshole to you online? Block them. Mute them. Realize that some people are only trying to get under your skin and evoke a response. You're probably going to disagree with at least fifty-percent of the people on the platform; don't fall into the productivity-killing time-suck. I also don't understand the compulsion some folks seem to have where they need to give their two cents on every single little nugget of news or headline that pops up on the *what's everyone mad about today* section of Twitter. Oh well. People are silly.

We all know those people who are only waiting for their turn to talk, and are not really invested in the overall conversation. That, from my perspective, is the perfect example of what social media is. Some people see it as their own personal Truman show, and they know they're the star.

I can't imagine being a kid nowadays, trying to navigate social media. The problems you might have at school could easily follow you around all day. The insecurities that you might feel could easily be exacerbated by the endless-scroll. The creeping idea that one's worth is measured by *likes* really weirds me out. It's becoming a little too *Black Mirror* for my taste.

Depression levels in pre-teens and teens are on the rise, and one of the biggest factors seems to be social media. As a new parent, these are things my wife and I will have to figure out. How can we ensure that our daughter doesn't value her own worth based on what she sees on the screen? How can we prevent her from falling victim to social media's culture of comparison? When do we allow her to join the ranks of social media, and how do we implement restrictions without coming off as controlling?

Social media seems like such a small and innocuous thing on the surface, but I truly believe that we have vastly underestimated its negative ramifications. The more I think about it, the more I find myself opposed to it, or at least trying to distance myself from its pull.

There are some positives about social media; although I don't know if the positives outweigh the negatives.

As for YouTube creators like me, social media is a powerful tool; almost a necessity. Interacting with followers is a rewarding experience, and announcing new videos or projects can keep people engaged.

That being said, I prefer interacting via live streams more than social media. Speaking to followers in a live chat is way more fun and interesting than typing something with my thumbs. If I manage my time wisely, avoid doing the endless-scroll dance, and only post when something is actually happening, then utilizing social media for the channel can be useful. As for non-HelloGreedo social media, apart from the few private groups I'm a part of with my oldest and lifelong friends, I don't have much of a desire.

CHAPTER 4
YOUTUBE

A lot of folks seem to think that there's some secret formula for having success on YouTube. There isn't. There's no formula. There's no *right way* to do things. There's no secret ten-step plan. Yes, tips and tricks can be given out, but it really just boils down to you making stuff that you would want to watch. That's it. Don't overthink it.

I have seen so many videos titled "HOW TO GET SUBSCRIBERS ON YOUTUBE!", and then when I check out the uploader's channel, they don't have any subscribers. Weird, right? You'd think that the person with all of the secrets would have a zillion subscribers! Right!? The real secret is that no one knows the secret. Everyone wants to tell you what to do. Most of it is just talk. I'll tell you what not to do. Or at least what I think isn't helpful. All you can do is harness your own personality, be yourself, speak your mind, and make stuff that you are personally proud of. That's it.

Stop focusing on your subscriber count. The measure of your channel should not be defined by the number of subscribers you have. If you focus on content, the subscribers will come organically. Kicking and screaming about a small subscriber count is doing a disservice to the subscribers you already have!

There is nothing more disengaging than a digital pity party. If you're unsatisfied by the reach you've achieved, try shifting your delivery method. Change things up. Appeal to a broader audience if you're focusing on a niche group, or focus on a niche group if you're appealing to a broader audience. Or just keep doing what you're doing. If what you're doing is making you happy, and you're satisfied with where you're at, there's no reason to change.

Just because one of your videos doesn't have the view count you're looking for, doesn't mean that you're doing anything wrong. It might just take time for it, and you, to be discovered by the viewership you're trying to attract. Like I said, there is no formula. The formula is you. Your personality and what you bring to the table is everything.

Never make a video begging for subscribers. Never comment on other people's videos telling people to check out your channel. Never tell people on a live stream chat to subscribe to your channel. Begging for subscribers isn't creating content. Begging for subscribers is like looking at YouTube as a video game, wanting to achieve some point-count by collecting the most shiny gold coins. The time people spend asking people to subscribe to their channel is time they should be spending making stuff that would want people to subscribe in the first place.

Notoriety shouldn't be your main goal. Notoriety comes after you have something to stand on. Don't let the idea of achieving a certain level of notoriety be what drives you. Just make stuff! There's a reason people make fun of reality stars. They're often famous without achievement. They seek fame for the sake of fame. The time you spend worrying about getting subscribers is time you could be spent making shit.

Don't compare yourself to other creators. Do you know how many times I've seen channels that started later than me surpass my viewership and subscriber count? A lot! Does it bother me? Not at all. It legitimately makes me happy. Competition is a great thing; it fuels innovation and creativity. But I have never once viewed YouTube, and my presence on it, as a competitive endeavor. If someone is presenting their content in a way that seems to be working for them, that's awesome! That doesn't mean that I need to shift the way that I do things. I like the way I do things. I enjoy making the content that I want to make.

My goal on YouTube isn't to achieve big beefy numbers, it's to be true to myself and say what I want to say. If I constantly compared myself to other people on the platform, my head wouldn't be in the game. Comparing yourself to other content creators is basically a digital version of keeping up with the Joneses. Wanting what others have. It's okay to compare yourself to other creators in terms of style and presentation, you might even get a little jolt of inspiration, but where things get squirrely is when comparison turns to envy. Those creators worked hard to get where they're at, and you have to work hard too. JUST MAKE STUFF!

Don't get discouraged. Everyone has writer's block. I view my channel as an ever-evolving presentation that I want to be proud of. Having this mindset has forced me to really think about what I'm uploading. I don't want filler. I don't want to force content. I don't want to be one of those creators who uploads twenty times a week. Every video that I upload is something that I am enthusiastic about, and something that I am proud of.

I have made dozens of videos that are saved on my computer, and they will never see the light of day. For one reason or another, I decided not to upload them. I might have viewed them as filler. I might have recognized that they weren't what I originally was going for. I might have decided to hold off until I get some new ideas to make the video better. I never want to feel rushed. I don't want to feel the heat of some deadline that I've arbitrarily put on myself. I want to make something polished that I am happy with.

Sometimes an idea takes months to flesh out,

and sometimes I can fully form an idea I'm happy with in a matter of minutes. Hell, my *Inside Star Wars – Revenge of the Sith* video took over a year to make. Not because I didn't want to make it, but because I didn't have any ideas I was happy with. I didn't want to force it. I wanted to be proud of it. So, on and off for a year I had an empty folder labeled *INSIDE ROTS* staring at me with nothing inside.

It's cool that a lot of channels upload daily, or have an extensive back catalogue of pre-made videos scheduled to release at certain intervals. I don't have that in me. If I did that, I honestly think I'd get burned out. It would turn something fun and enjoyable into something that felt like scheduled work. Of course, taking my time isn't what gets the ad revenue flowing on YouTube. More uploads equals more money. Why do you think so many people just turn on their webcam a few times a day, and talk about the latest and greatest trending or controversial topics? The monetization of outrage towards the most petty and inconsequential things has become an industry in itself on YouTube.

There's never a reason to feel like you have to copy what other channels are doing by uploading daily. You can take your time too. The ideas will come when they come.

In the past, when a new trailer or nugget of news dropped, I felt pressured to immediately hop on the computer and start making a video. Not anymore. I often sleep on it and let the information soak in my brain overnight. I've found that my opinions, observations, or even arguments are better after they have a little time to marinade. I do not feel the need to be the first person to comment on something like I did in the past. Being first is no longer important to me.

YouTube is a platform for expressing who you truly are. People watch YouTube, and subscribe to certain creators, because of authenticity. Unlike many other forms of entertainment, there's no middleman between the creator and the audience. If someone is watching your video, they are seeing something that came directly out of your head. There are no executives pulling strings on what can and can't be said. There's no advertising committee breaking down demographics. So, be yourself. Be the self that you are when you are surrounded by your best friends. Unfiltered. Unhinged. Unabashed in your thoughts. You have the freedom to hand something completely authentic to the world. Say what you want to say, and say it in your own unique way.

I've seen YouTube turn introverts into extroverts, and extroverts into ambiverts. The platform tends to make people a little more open and expressive than they normally would be if the cameras weren't rolling. There seems to be a propensity for being a little more verbose than one would normally be outside of YouTube. It makes sense. There's nothing wrong with it. Turn up the dial and flow with it.

Then again, would you really scream, yell and wallow around if you were playing a video game alone in your room? Probably not. Whenever I see live streams like that, I tune out.

Would you really scream and yell if you were watching a movie trailer alone in your living room? I doubt it. So, why fake it? Aren't reactions supposed to be real? I usually watch trailers when I'm on the toilet.

Don't feel like you have to agree with your viewers. I find this to be a very important point. It is inevitable that if you put out an opinion that differs from the majority, you will receive a whole bunch of negative feedback. That's fine. Accept it. Embrace it. The most important thing about your channel, and keeping your sanity, is being completely authentic. Just because the majority likes something, doesn't mean you have to like it. Just because the majority dislikes something, doesn't mean you have to dislike it.

Sometimes it can be a fun experience to have your opinion fall in the minority. It forces you to flesh out your opinions, and encourages you to strengthen your arguments. Having a different opinion than the vast majority of your viewership can also be a learning experience. You can hear what they have to say, and interact with them on an interesting level. Friendly discourse is fun.

My friend once asked me if I felt pressured to agree with my viewers. I replied with a quick "no". If I'm making a video, that means I have something I want to say. It doesn't mean that I want to parrot and repeat the feelings of others just for the sake of appeasement and agreement. Life is easy when everyone agrees, but it's not fun. It's boring. It's important to remain respectful, though. You have to recognize that everyone's tastes are different. There's no reason to put anyone down if they like a movie that you don't like. That's a goofy way to interact with people. When people discuss their disagreement on certain topics it can be enjoyable, informative, and educational. But when someone acts like an asshole, you might as well be talking to a goddamn wall.

Don't dwell on the negative comments. This is one that took me a while to come to terms with, and advice that I often need to remember. I could receive one-hundred positive comments and words of encouragement, but as soon as one negative comment came in, I immediately focused on it. Why? What is it about a slice of negatively that forced itself into my brain like that weird-ass-dumb-mind-reading octopus from *Rogue One*? It used to be very difficult to dispel negative comments from my attention. Sometimes they sting, and sometimes you sit back wondering if the person on the other end of the conversation is being authentic or just a troll trying to get a rise out of you. That's a real thing too; social media accounts with zero followers, zero posts, and no avatar spamming you with the most inane nonsense, just hoping you respond. Just ignore it. It's not worth the effort. Trolls are real. The longer you shine your flashlight on them the bigger and bolder they grow.

A lot of people seem to think the phrase *don't feed the trolls* is a bad thing. They see not engaging with troll as being an *apologist* or an *enabler*. I don't see it that way at all. Some people spend their time navigating the internet with a goal of pissing people off and stirring shit up. They'll send the same message to hundreds of people, and hope they can get a response. What's the point of engaging them? If you get flustered and send a super-mad Twitter tirade their way, they see that as win. Fuck 'em. Ignore it. You should be able to tell the different between when someone is honestly disagreeing with you, and when someone is just trying to piss you off. It's not the same thing. Don't get it confused.

Like I said, it took me a long time to overcome the fear of, or even the desire to retaliate against, negative comments. Negativity for the sake of negativity is a trait you should run away from. Who needs that shit in their life?

When trolls find a weakness, they exploit it. When they find a soft spot, they poke. At the same time, recognize that constructive criticism can be extremely valuable. There's a big difference between outright negativity, and constructive criticism. It's easy to confuse the two, especially when your heart and soul goes into a project and someone is innocently giving you pointers with no malicious intent. A friendly suggestion can easily be taken the wrong way, especially in this new age of digital communication. It's difficult to interpret tone and intent via text.

Don't feel obligated to follow the trends. It happens all too often; as soon as a huge channel releases a video based on a new concept, a ton of smaller channels follow suit and copy that video's concept. There's really nothing wrong with that, it plays into meme culture, I suppose. But if the habit is formed it may make your channel look like it doesn't produce any original content. Of course, I do see the positive side of this. Viewers searching around on YouTube for a specific video concept might stumble onto your channel, and click that super-holy-sacred-omg subscribe button. I get it. That could potentially get new eyeballs on your work. But I personally think that originality should always trump the trends. Especially when thousands of people are doing the exact same thing, your video might just get lost in the noise. Do your own thing. Make the trends.

If you choose to remain anonymous, use your anonymity for good. Anyone can hide behind a keyboard, or wear a mask like myself, and be an asshole. It's tempting, right? *No one knows who I am! I have carte blanche to be a total dick!* I can't stress the authentic-self enough when creating and maintaining your channel. Talk to people online as if you were talking to them face to face.

When I do decide to poke fun of something, I tend to poke fun of practices, not people. I don't overtly make satire about individuals; I'd rather make satire about practices, hyperbole, and clickbait. It's more fun and doesn't feel personal; it is never personal. If I make a satire video making fun of creators who claim to have *inside sources* or *leaks,* I rarely do it with any one person in mind. It's more of an amalgamation of numerous creators or websites who I think are being silly gooses.

I suppose these tips kind of focus on channels that are already made and looking to establish a voice. What if you don't have a channel at all and you're looking to get your foot in the door?

So, maybe you've been bouncing the idea of creating a YouTube channel from scratch in your head. Or maybe you haven't, and this chapter will make you want to make one!

What should your first step be? I'd recommend sitting down and typing up a game plan. Just toss together some ideas and make an overall outline of what you want to accomplish. There are no dumb ideas. There are no embarrassing subject matters. Find what interests you the most, and roll with it.

I was very apprehensive about making a Star Wars YouTube Channel, because I was worried about how it was going to be received. Looking back, I shouldn't have been worried at all. There's an audience for anything and everything.

Personality and presentation are the two most important things in my opinion. There are a billion YouTube channels that focus on video games. It's a more saturated market than homemade beaded jewelry on Etsy. So, if you're going to make a video game channel, what's going to set you apart? How are you going to present your ideas? What is going to make your video game channel different than the incalculable amount of video game channels on the platform?

Oh! This should have been the very first thing I put in this chapter, because it might be the most important. Do not do it for the money. If your main goal is to be able to do YouTube full time, and make it your primary source of income, don't hold your breath. I've been on YouTube for almost 8 years now, and it's only recently become a decent source of income. When I say decent, I mean that the channel pays for my mortgage. That fact is all thanks to patrons and sponsors, of course. I couldn't do it without their support. Ad revenue is incredibly unreliable, and I want to avoid having thirty-second sponsored ads build into the meat of my videos.

It's been a long road. The channel has gone through lot of ups and downs, as well as discouraging and encouraging moments. So, start your YouTube channel for fun, because when you're having fun and not focusing on the monetization, that's when the true freedom and creativity shines through. Just have fun. The money may or may not come. It probably won't.

I find that there's no method to the madness. The videos I think will get me a lot of views and a decent payday end up making me $20 after 7 hours of work. The videos I think people will consider filler and not want to watch end up making me $100 that day. For a channel my size that targets a small audience in comparison to the overall YouTube user base, revenue is completely unpredictable and often relies on outside events, news, and topical information. I kind of lucked out. I made my channel in 2011, well before Disney acquired Star Wars. There's just a lot more to talk about now.

If you're aspiring to grow a YouTube channel over a few years, you absolutely need a strong work ethic. Doing YouTube full time has probably been, other than the Navy, the most time consuming, nerve-racking, and enjoyable *job* I've ever had. There's no security in it. If you take a week off, there's no sick pay. Taxes are a son of a bitch to figure out. The days are long. There's a lot of moving parts and communication. I've without a doubt put more work hours into HelloGreedo than anything else. But I built it. That's the difference. I can sit back and be proud of the thing that I made. It's incredibly rewarding. It's the definition of personal freedom. It's indescribably fulfilling.

Occasionally a channel will explode overnight, gaining an insane following in the blink of an eye. Sometimes things just work out. The stars align. They hit their stride fast, and find their groove. That's extremely rare. The vast majority of YouTubers worked years to get where they're at. They honed their skills over time, found their groove by trial and error, and slowly gained notoriety. So, prepare for that. Work hard and kick ass. You never know where you might end up.

I get asked about equipment a lot. There seems to be this idea out there that you need some beefy camera or microphone to start a YouTube channel. That is absolutely not true. I started my channel with a cheap point and shoot camera and a $15 headset microphone. You already have everything you need to get started. Hell, your phone is an all-in-one YouTube creator studio. Experiment with it.

Something I never imagined I'd get into was streaming, but I did. Sometime in 2017 I started streaming a lot. Interacting with everyone, playing games with followers, and being completely off the cuff became incredibly fun. It was a nice change of pace; my videos are completely scripted, so I found it thrilling to go live with an audience and have no idea what topic of conversation would come up.

When I stream a video game, the stream is less about the video game than it is about me just shooting the shit with the audience. The game itself is almost background noise; just something to keep the flow going, and have something on screen.

I couldn't be one of those streamers that plays a game for a few hours, only looking at the chat between rounds and barely interacting with the audience. Hell, I don't have a desire to watch streamers like that. I don't get it. Streaming, to me, is more like a podcast than anything. Like I said, it's less about the game and more about just hanging out.

It's never too early to start streaming. If your channel is brand new and you only have a few videos uploaded, add streaming into the mix! It can bring in an entirely new audience that you hadn't thought of reaching out to. Also, don't think of streaming as just playing video games. You can treat it as an interview platform, a podcast, or anything else you'd like. Hell, you could go live and do a headstand for an hour. Actually, that's not a bad idea. I'm surprised I haven't heard of any streamers doing dumb shit like that. Maybe it exists, but I haven't seen it. *Watch me brush my teeth for an hour! Watch me do jumping jacks for an hour! Watch me dribble a basketball for an hour!* There's definitely a market for that kind of goofy stuff.

In all seriousness, streaming has surprisingly been one of the most rewarding things I've done on the channel. It's a way to instantly connect with the people who watch my stuff. I'm able to talk to people from all around globe, in real-time, about whatever we want. It's even been an amazing way to improve my communication skills. I've been challenged on live streams before, and forced to convey my opinions without having much time to prepare my thoughts. It has been an incredibly rewarding experience. To everyone who has ever tuned into my live streams, thank you for being a part of the fun.

Look, I got lucky. I started a *Star Wars* YouTube channel when YouTube was in its infancy, and at that time there weren't many people exclusively talking about *Star Wars*. I started the channel before Disney acquired the franchise. I started the channel before anyone ever imagined new *Star Wars* movies would be made. The initial flash of success that the channel received was the perfect example of being in the right place at the right time.

Now there are countless *Star Wars* YouTube channels. I can't imagine trying to be heard in a sea of similar voices. I will always credit *luck* as the main reason for the minor success of *HelloGreedo*.

CHAPTER 5
MY TEN FAVORITE MOVIES

There's a very short list of things that I love more than going to see a movie. Every time I plop my ass down in the theater, I am greeted with a new experience. I'm always hit with a sense of wonder and adventure when the lights slowly vanish, and the screen fades to black. Will I be taken on an emotional roller coaster, or will my knuckles turn white from gripping the seat during a suspenseful action scene? Will I shed a tear during moments of heroic triumph, or will my gut bust from hilarity? Every movie is a blank canvas waiting to be painted by your impressions.

Sometimes movies can be so much more than a singular theater experience. Movies have the ability to stick with you for your entire life. That's why this list was so difficult for me to put together, and I probably shouldn't have even made this chapter. I have a lot of *favorite* movies, but a few stand out more than others. What these ten movies all have in common are characters that I love and stories that I find satisfying. Most of the movies on this list are ones that I grew up watching, and they left a huge impression on me.

These ten movies aren't in any particular order, and I predict that a few years from now this list will be completely different. My list of top ten favorite movies is always changing. I left any *Star Wars* movies off the list, because *duh*.

Looking at this list I realized it is painfully obviously that I was born in the 80s and grew up in the 90s.

The Right Stuff (1983)
Directed by Philip Kaufman

The Right Stuff holds a very special place in my heart. The movie touches on my lifelong enthusiasm for space exploration, astronomy, and history. *The Right Stuff* is the story of the Mercury 7, America's first astronauts. The viewer is taken on a ride through the selection process, the emotional toil of an astronaut's family, the heroic achievements of everyone involved, the blossoming of friendships, the tension built between departments, the demands of media coverage, and the bond forged through brotherhood.

The Right Stuff is not only a story about triumph in the face of the unknown; it's also a really funny movie. When cocky, highly competitive, and overconfident test pilots from different branches of the military come in contact with one another, bravado fills the room like perfume in a department store. They were the best of the best, and they knew it.

It's impossible for me to pick a single all-time favorite movie, but if I had to choose just one, *The Right Stuff* might be at the top of the pyramid. Go watch it.

Good Will Hunting (1997)
Directed by Gus Van Sant

I love small and focused stories; stories that show a central character's evolution through interaction and experience; stories that aren't muddied by too many faces and names to remember. A movie that never strays too far from the narrative's ultimate goal is a movie that I will at least appreciate, and it may even leave a lifelong impression. *Good Will Hunting* is one of those movies.

Good Will Hunting was written by Matt Damon and Ben Affleck. Will Hunting, the movie's main character, is a janitor at M.I.T. He is an undiscovered mathematical genius who isn't sure of himself, and tries his best to hide his abilities. He has no direction. His future is questionable.

I love *Good Will Hunting* because it's a story about discovering yourself. It's a story about emulating your environment, and being too afraid of the unknown to fulfill the greatness you are capable of. The friendships found between characters in the film feel one-hundred-percent genuine. The bond between Will Hunting and the psychologist Sean

Maguire is touching. Sean becomes the father figure that Will always needed. Will Hunting's friend Chuckie, played by Ben Affleck, is one of the most realistic friendships I've ever seen on screen. Probably because they're good friends in real life. *Good Will Hunting* is one of those types of movies I can watch over and over again, and never get sick of.

Apollo 13 (1995)
Directed by Ron Howard

Another one of my soft spots are selfless acts of heroism in the face of nearly impossible odds. It's funny, I rarely tear up during a sad part of a movie, but I always tear up during moments of triumph. When Gene Kranz (Played by Ed Harris) sits down in the chair when it's realized that the astronauts are home safe, he sheds a tear. He wipes his face. The effort to get three men home safe was a success. It gets me every time.

Apollo 13 is the perfect true story to be made into a film, and the way Ron Howard captured the spirit of the adventure is brilliant. Astronauts are some of the most complex and interesting characters you can have in a movie. Sure, all of their personalities differ, but they all exemplify the fighting spirit, a sense of self sacrifice, and an unshakable duty towards the pursuit of knowledge and discovery. Oh, and most of them are cocky as shit. Wouldn't you be too? I know I'm romanticizing astronauts a little too much, but they are my heroes.

Ron Howard establishes the characters in *Apollo 13* perfectly. By bringing the families of the astronauts into the story, another layer of tension is created. The audience feels their pain, and roots for the crew of Apollo 13 even more.

Apollo 13 isn't just a story about astronauts and NASA; it's a story about the human spirit. When people come together forging the grounds of a common goal, great things can be accomplished. When humans are in need, humans come to the rescue.

127 Hours (2011)
Directed by Danny Boyle

The most deep seated animalistic instinct we all possess is the will to survive. The lengths we are all capable of to ensure we don't let the lights go out. Eat, drink, sleep, pass our DNA to the next generation, and *fight or flight*. But what if you are physically unable to move and flight is not an option? What if there's nothing to fight other than your own psyche and determination to survive?

127 Hours is the true story of Aron Ralston's will to live. With his arm pinned against a canyon wall by an immovable boulder, he is tested in ways that none of us could ever imagine. The film is a journey through a man's mind who is running out of time; limited supplies, bitter cold temperatures, and extreme isolation.

What I always hear from people who haven't seen *127 Hours* is, "I already know the ending" or "I don't want to see someone cut their own arm off". The movie is so much deeper than a story about a man who cuts off his arm. It's about triumphing in the face of certain death, and saying *fuck this, I'm going to live.*

No matter how many times I watch *127 Hours,* I always find myself with a big lump in my throat at the end. The song *Festival* by Sigur Rós that plays at the end definitely influences that lump.

Saving Private Ryan (1998)
Directed by Steven Spielberg

What makes a good war movie? It's not the explosions or action. It's not the rattling of machine gun fire or the portrayal of gruesome violence. What makes a good war movie is the same thing that makes any good movie; characters. Characters that are put in situations that test their morality, their patience, and as Captain Miller says, their ability to "*follow fucking orders*".

Saving Private Ryan is so much more than just a movie; it's a realistic window that allows us to peer into the world's most bloody, costly, and harrowing war. I was lucky enough to see *Saving Private Ryan* in the movie theater when I was twelve years old. World War 2 veterans were sitting all around me. From the very first scene, they were weeping. That's when I knew this movie was different. This wasn't Rambo. This was real. This was lived. *Saving Private Ryan* is a movie that begs the world to never forget the sacrifice of those who stared evil in the face. It begs the world to remember the tyranny of Nazi Germany, and those who gave their life to see Hitler's swastika turned to ash.

The downtime that we spend with each character allows the audience to get to know them. We see their internal struggles, and we learn about where they came from. Establishing characters in a movie about war gives us the ability to empathize with a soldier on a human level. It makes us grieve their loss, and gain a greater appreciation for their sacrifice.

So, when I said I was hoping *Rogue One* was going to be like *Saving Private Ryan* in one of my videos, I wasn't talking about bang bang boom boom. I was talking about capturing the horrors of war and the characters that find themselves in it. That's where *Rogue One* fell short for me. I wasn't invested in the characters.

Back to the Future (1985)
Directed by Robert Zemeckis

Is there a more fun movie than *Back to the Future*? I really don't think so. It's goofy, clever, incredibly well written, and it's fun. On paper, I don't know if the movie makes much sense. An old white-haired scientist who befriends a high school boy who ends up going back in time and becoming friends with his dad and has to deflect his mother's lust? Yeah, that sounds pretty weird. It doesn't seem like something that would work, but it does!

Back to the Future is as timeless as a movie can get. I can't imagine a day where it no longer holds up. A great movie tends to stand the test of time because of a great story. *Back to the Future* has a great story with a heavy dose of great characters. It doesn't bog itself down with the need to explain time travel in some convoluted way; Marty just goes back in time. No explanation needed. Just watch it and have fun.

Marty McFly, as a character, is someone we can all relate to. He's a teenager with big ambitions and dreams. He wants that shiny black four wheel truck. He wants the girl. His immaturity and ignorance isn't annoying; it's kind of charming.

More than anything, *Back to the Future* is just plain delightful. Silly characters and a silly plot make for one of the most enjoyable movies I can think of. The sequels are great too, but they don't nearly have the same impact on me as the original. I loved watching the second movie when I was a kid because I enjoyed the futuristic aspects of it; hoverboards, weird clothes, flying cars, videos games, etc. The hyper-80s version of the future is one that I've always loved.

Men in Black (1997)
Directed by Barry Sonnenfeld

I was eleven years old when *Men in Black* came out. Eleven is probably the perfect age to see the movie. I remember being completely blown away by how alive the movie made the world of MIB feel; how believable and imaginative it was.

Many of the scenes remind me of the Mos Eisley Cantina in *A New Hope*, especially when we find ourselves in the MIB headquarters. We watch strange aliens walk around a bustling space-port, all while the global population of Earth is in the dark. Will Smith's endless charisma, mixed with Tommy Lee Jones' dryness, is the perfect combination.

The movie doesn't take itself too serious, and everything is continuously rooted in fish-out-of-water comedy. I constantly quote *Men In Black* for some reason. Whether it's lines of dialogue like *"sugar, in water"* or *"this definitely rates about a 9.0 on my weird-shit-o-meter"* or *"we're not hosting an intergalactic kegger"*. It's a goofy movie with a goofy premise and a goofy cast.

I'm a big fan of science fiction, and *Men in Black* splices science fiction with that grade-A 90s Will Smith comedy that we all loved so much. I still remember seeing the movie in the theater. It kind of blew my mind. I love it, and it's without a doubt one of the movies I'm most excited to show my daughter.

Oh, and I owned the hell out of the *Men in Black* soundtrack.

Jaws (1975)
Steven Spielberg

Every July I get into *Jaws is my favorite movie of all time* mode. That might be true. My wife and I have a tradition where we watch the movie on our projector in the backyard every summer.

I personally think it's one of the best made movies, and one of the scariest movies without being directly labeled as a *horror* movie. Hell, it's way scarier than most horror movies.

Brody, Hooper, and Quint make up the perfect trio. Each have extremely unique qualities that make up their character. Brody is the every-man, the do-gooder, your friendly neighbor. But the true show stealer is Robert Shaw as Quint. Quint truly makes the second half of the movie.

One of the aspects of *Jaws* I've always appreciated is how subtly used the shark was. It's well documented that the giant mechanical shark often broke down, and that definitely helped the movie in the long run. When we float in the ocean and look below, it evokes an eerie feeling in real life. The unknown and mystery of what lurks below is a feeling I think we've all felt, and *Jaws* does a fantastic job of capturing that feeling and putting it on screen.

The use of musical cues is one of the strong points as well. When the shark is near, we hear the repetitive march of John Williams' score. When the shark is not present, the music is often mute. The best example of this is when the kids are swimming around and pranking the beachgoers. The audience swims through the water from their perspective. We assume that we're about to witness something gruesome. The giveaway is the lack of music. It's a brilliant auditory way to hint at true danger in the film. *Jaws* is a masterpiece.

Indiana Jones (1981, 1984, 1989)
Steven Spielberg

I can't pick a favorite Indiana Jones film. I love the first three for entirely different reasons. *Raiders of the Lost Ark* is slow paced. *Temple of Doom* is a silly romp. *The Last Crusade* kind of meshes the two previous movies, and creates a broad and wild adventure.

Growing up, I definitely watched *Temple of Doom* more than the other two. I don't remember liking it more than the others, but for whatever reason it was the one that always seemed readily available. My family had a mini-van with TVs, and whenever we went on road trips we'd always pop in *Temple of Doom*. I'd say the general consensus is that it's the weakest of the three. I don't necessarily agree with that; it's just different. See, I came to the party late. I was born in 1986. If I was old enough to see *Raiders* in the theater in 1981, and then *Temple of Doom* came out, I can imagine being disappointed with it. I love *Temple*. Honestly, it might be my favorite.

The Last Crusade, like I said, takes elements from the two previous films and meshes them so well. It is often serious in tone, but adds a dash of silliness to even it out. To me, it's more adventurous than the other two. The film often ping-pongs around various locations at a rapid pace, as our heroes bicker, discover, and get into sticky situations. The relationship between father and son is perfect.

My heart likes *Temple* and *Crusade* more than *Raiders,* but my head likes *Raiders* more than *Temple* and *Crusade*. I have to follow my heart.

Indiana Jones, as a character, isn't anything extraordinarily deep. His character is more of an image, an attitude, a general sense of wanting to do the right thing and kick some ass while doing it. There's no question why kids wanted to be Indiana Jones; don a fedora, pretend to fight bad guys, and explore the backyard.

The Matrix (1999)
The Wachowskis

I never saw *The Matrix* in the theater. In fact, I don't think I had ever heard of *The Matrix* until it was available on DVD.

I was hanging out with my friends one day, and my dad came home from work with a copy of the movie. I remember him telling me I should watch it because he thought I'd like it. Boy oh boy, was he right.

The Matrix might've seemed like far-fetched science fiction when it came out in 1999, but twenty years later, in the year 2019, it seems believable. The more humanity learns about the brain, artificial intelligence, and virtual reality, it seems more likely than ever that one day we will have a virtual experience indistinguishable from reality.

I loved the concept of humanity being nothing more than a battery to fuel the robots that took over the world, while the robots create a virtual world for us to live in. How nice of them! Thank you robots! The story was, on all fronts, incredibly interesting, engaging, and fun. It is a sleek trench coat action flick layered over a pretty deep and philosophical story. The action was mind-blowing at the time, and really changed the game for what would come in the genre.

I can't tell you how excited I was for the sequels, and how disappointed I was in them. The second *Matrix* movie wasn't too bad; I liked a lot of ideas in it. But the third movie…damn. I remember walking out of the theater with my buddy Matt, sitting down for a late night hamburger, and talking about how much we hated it.

As a kid who was so deeply invested in computers, PC gaming, and everything in that culture at the time, *The Matrix* spoke to me on a whole bunch of levels.

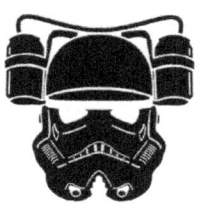

So, those are my ten favorite movies. Actually, no they're not. This list could change tomorrow. It will change tomorrow. Hell, I should have put *Jurassic*

Park somewhere in there. *Jurassic Park* definitely beats out *The Matrix*. Well, maybe not. It definitely beats out *127 Hours* thought. Shit, maybe not. I could think of a dozen other movies that should have been on this list. What the hell was the point of this chapter? I should have known it would be impossible to pick a top ten movies list. Rip this chapter out of the book and throw it in the garbage!

What I find hilarious is how obvious it is that I was a kid who grew up in the 90s. This list probably parallels so many lists from people my age. It's also painfully obvious that Spielberg owns my soul.

CHAPTER 6
THE UNITED STATES NAVY

When channel viewers find out that their friendly neighborhood YouTube Stormtrooper was in the military, they're often surprised. On the other hand, whenever I find out that someone was in the military, I'm never surprised. I served with people from all walks of life.

I deployed with dudes who would play *Magic the Gathering* in the galley, and I deployed with gym rats who wanted to come home looking like Captain America. I deployed with photographers, musicians, math-wizards, tech-geeks, football fanatics, and foreigners serving to gain citizenship. I served with every type of human being you can think of. Some people, it seems, have a specific idea of what a service member looks and acts like. *A guy in the military can't be a Star Wars nerd!* Well, if you think that, then you probably haven't been in the military.

So, I'm never surprised when I find out that someone served. The smartest people I've ever met, I met in the United States Navy. By the same token, the dumbest people I've ever met, I met in the United States Navy. The Navy is like anywhere else; all different types of people. People always seem to talk about diversity; they need to look no further than the United States Navy. It's a giant cultural blender stuffed with human-salad that produces all-natural, gluten-free, farm-to-table camaraderie.

I really can't sit down and write a book about me and my thoughts without including a chapter about my time in the military. It was the biggest decision I ever made in my life, and aside from marrying my wife and becoming a father, the most important. Not to mention a lot of young folks tell me they're thinking about enlisting. I feel obligated to present my experience and give my honest advice.

The military is not for everyone. I can't stress that enough. Yes, human beings are fantastic at adapting to situations, but some people aren't meant for the military. You could also flip that statement and say the military isn't meant for them. Those statements are not meant to be degrading in any way; everyone is different. That's why I am strongly against forcing kids into joining the military, unless it's some form of mandatory national service; an idea I don't know if I'm opposed to or in favor of. Do some kids need structure and discipline? You bet. Hell, I needed structure and discipline, but I didn't enlist until I was 21. I discovered, on my own, that I was in desperate need of structure and discipline.

Just because Captain Dad served in the military doesn't mean that Billy Boy needs to serve too. You're not doing the fleet a service by forcing your kid to join. You might be adding a bitter non-volunteer to an all-volunteer military, and that's not good for anyone.

Before the military, I was constantly unsure of myself. I rarely followed through with personal goals, and my indecisiveness ran rampant. I could never pick a path. I let my anxiety get the best of me. I felt directionless, disconnected, and useless. Watching all of my friends thrive in college made me question my own abilities, and I would often find myself in an existential funk. *What am I doing wrong? Why am I not motivated? Why can't I just buckle down and finish school?*

My home life was amazing; two extremely supportive and loving parents, a sister who is a saint, an extended family that's closer than any I've ever seen, the best school district in the state of Florida, and upper-middle class suburbia. The tools for success were always at my disposal. The problems I had were my own.

Despite years without direction, and being tentative about every decision I made, I was the easiest sell my recruiter ever had to make. I had zero hesitation about enlisting. I pulled an all-nighter the day before I went to the recruiter, and was standing outside of their door the second they opened in the morning. I pretty much walked right into the recruiter's office, told her I wanted to enlist, and signed the paperwork. I made meeting her quota super easy that month.

Looking back, I think the reason I enlisted without question was that I needed to be a part of something that gave me no wiggle room. Whenever I was given wiggle room, I'd always find excuses and find a way out. Enlisting provided me an opportunity where saying *no* was not an option; I forced myself to be forced into sticking something out. I signed on the dotted line and was happy to have the next four years be plotted out for me.

I went to boot camp in 2007, and quickly discovered that I liked being regimented and moving fast. The sound of my RDC (*Recruit Division Commanders. What the Navy calls their Drill Instructors*) busting into the berthing at 0500 became comforting. They'd scream until we were all standing perfectly still at the end of our bunks, and would proceed to throw chairs around the room if we were too slow. After we'd all been verbally abused, we were given fifteen minutes to shit, shower, and shave.

Let me rewind a bit. My family dropped me off at a hotel, I hopped on a flight the next morning with a bunch of other recruits, we flew to Chicago, hopped on a bus, and arrived at Recruit Training Command, Great Lakes, Illinois that night. That day had been a complete whirlwind. In retrospect, I shouldn't have been nervous at all, but I was. I only really got nervous when our bus reached the gate of the base. That's when it really sunk in that my life was about to temporarily change.

The first week of boot camp is full of what are called *P-Days*. You spend those days being processed by medical, dental, fulfilling all of the administrative requirements, learning how to stand watch, march, and function in this heavily regimented world.

The most vivid memory I have of those first few days was when my division went to get our medical shots. Like an assembly line, we all walked forward, not stopping, as a dozen or so medical personnel stood on either side of us, sticking us with needles. It looked like something out of a horror movie.

Every day was devoted to exercise, classroom activity, and training. After a while, the routine became second nature. I found myself loving the long runs, the marching, and the routine. Standing watch for four hours in the dead of night became a time of self-reflection. Everything that I was initially unsure of became relaxing. Humans are good at adapting. After a week or two being in this hyper-organized world, I found myself missing home less and less, but as my division's graduation day got closer, I became more homesick. The light at the end of the tunnel was creeping closer, and I had no idea where I'd end up next.

Before boot camp, I had a fair amount of social anxiety. Inside of boot camp, that anxiety completely disappeared. I had no hesitation to walk up to one of my fellow recruits and spark up a conversation. I had no problem asking for help, or helping others if I saw them struggling. The experience stripped me down to my studs, and rebuilt me with the knowledge that we are all the same. People are just people.

Despite all the horror stories and nonsense you read on the internet, boot camp is relatively easy. Shut up, do what you're told, and be a sponge that's ready to absorb information. That's it. I'm sure it's changed quite a bit since I went, but I'd be willing to bet that those three tips still apply. Millions of people have gone through it; there's no reason to be scared. The public has an odd fascination with boot camp. I spent four years in the Navy, and the main questions I get usually revolve around the first few weeks that I spent in boot camp. Strange.

Boot camp was also absolutely hilarious. All of us would be standing in front of our bunks, as our Chief paced and yelled in the middle of the room, and the guys across from you would try to make one another laugh. It was never a conscious decision, or a discussion we all had with one another. But when Chief turned his back towards our side of the room, and faced the guys on the other side, we'd hump the air and try to get them to laugh. Or make really stupid faces. Just dumb shit. It was fun. If you started laughing, or were caught doing dumb shit, the entire division would pay for it. The punishment was worth it for a little bit of humor and normalcy.

As weird as it may seem, pranks were a thing in boot camp. One of the go-to classics was to, in the middle of the night, sneak over to someone's rack (bed) and tie their boots to the metal leg. When the RDCs busted in the room in the morning, everyone would be scurrying around, trying to get dressed and stand at attention as quick as possible ... and there you are ... boots knotted fifteen times around your rack ... trying to figure out how the hell you were going to get out of this without being yelled at. You'd never tattle. You'd just do something else to them the next night. It helped pass the time, and it kept things fun for everyone. Some recruits had a really hard time adapting. It's your duty to try and boost their spirit. Sometimes that means doing dumb pranks.

Everything in boot camp is meant to cultivate a feeling of teamwork. Whether it be the gas chamber, long runs, swim qualification, or the closing event called *Battle Stations*, it is all meant to instill the Navy virtue of *One Team, One Fight*.

Overall, boot camp was a lot easier than I expected. Its main purpose is to instill a routine. It aims to teach you discipline, teamwork, and the Navy's core values. Looking back, I kind of see my time at boot camp as a mental reset and a personal test. I needed it.

When a recruit completes boot camp, depending on their rate (job), they are usually sent to *A School*. *A School* is basically a condensed vocational college. You are sent to learn your specific job. My *A School* was in the small town of Meridian, Mississippi.

A School was both awesome and strange at

the same time. It's awesome because you're given more privileges and freedom than in boot camp, and you earn more privileges as you progress through your studies and stay out of trouble. The experience was a lot like college. Everyone stayed in what could be compared to dorms, attended classes all day, and had free time in the evening. The space I lived in had four people to a room, with four rooms, and a common area in the center. When we were done with our studies and duties, my roommates and I would sometimes hang out in the common area and play video games.

My favorite memories of *A School* involve a lake, some beer, a charcoal grill, a can of chewing tobacco, and hamburgers. Whenever the weekend rolled around, that's what my buddies and I would do; fire up the lakeside grill and hang out. After the organization and discipline of boot camp, *A School* felt unhinged and rowdy, which it certainly was not. It just felt that way.

Truthfully, my *A School* felt like a big waste of time and government money. The things I learned in the classroom could have easily been learned hands-on in the fleet. I'm a hands-on learner, and I learn best in the environment where I'll be doing the work. That being said, it was fun, and it served the purpose of slowly acclimating you back to the regular world after boot camp.

I never quite put my finger on why *A School* felt strange. It felt more like a summer camp than a military base. Kids would arrive straight out of boot camp, marching in their uniform, being uber-disciplined; and then there'd be kids who had been there for a few months, earned the privilege of wearing civilian clothes, and going off base to the local mall. It was such an interesting mix of relaxation and regulation.

Our school had a Marine Master Sergeant overseeing a lot of the day to day operations. I'm not sure exactly what his official role was at the school, but everyone knew him for the morning PT he conducted. All of the students would pour out at 0500, line up, and run nine miles with Master Sergeant at the lead. At the halfway mark, we'd come across a football field and fireman carry one another back and forth across it. The run would take place in the woods, on trails, and on the road. Master Sergeant would bring his dog to run alongside us.

That morning run was the type of thing I'd bitch and moan about in the moment, but in hindsight, it was an amazing character and teamwork building exercise. It taught me to keep pushing. It also taught me some fun cadences to hum in my head whenever I go on a jog.

> *Little yellow birdie with a little yellow bill*
> *Landed on my window sill*
> *Lured him in with a piece of bread*
> *Shut the fucking window*
> *And smashed his fucking head*

Obviously, no one would hurt a little yellow birdie with a little yellow bill. But damn, the Marines have the best songs, and some really good singers.

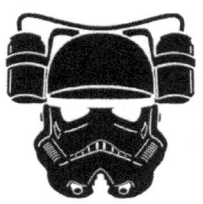

My first two years in the fleet were spent on shore duty, and it was like any other job. What made it feel even more like any other job was the fact that I got stationed in Jacksonville, Florida, and I'm from Jacksonville, Florida. Ridiculous, right? Join the Navy; see the world. Truthfully, I wasn't complaining. I was actually pushing for it. Jacksonville was one of the places I put on the list of places I'd like to get stationed, and I got it. I was excited to come back home. I loved where I grew up, and I wasn't running away from anything. I was a little homesick, after all. Also, If it wasn't for the fact that I got stationed in Jacksonville I probably wouldn't have started dating my now wife, and we wouldn't have our super snuggly baby daughter!

So, yeah, it felt like any other job for the first two years. Get to work at 0600, and go home at 1500. Stand watch for four hour chunks once a month. It was fun, but relatively uneventful. My job was to catalogue helicopter components, calculate engine hours, schedule maintenance, and make sure the numerous aircraft at our squadron maintained a constant state of readiness.

During the two years of shore duty, I'd occasionally get called to perform base security duties as part of the Auxiliary Security Force. This meant firearms training, room clearing drills, and getting pepper sprayed while running a hand-to-hand combat obstacle course with my eyes welded shut. It was a blast!

Getting pepper sprayed is without a doubt the most painful experience I've ever had. Some of the other people who were sprayed functioned way better than I did. It affected me for well over twenty-four hours. On the drive home, I had to stop at my friend's house and hold my eyes open underneath his bathtub faucet. My reaction to getting sprayed went from extreme pain, to extreme anger, back to extreme pain. When I gathered my composure and began focusing on the obstacle course, I got super pissed. I'll have to dig up the video sometime and show you guys.

After my two years on shore duty were over, I was switched over to sea duty at the same squadron. This pretty much meant that I could be deployed at any time.

In October of 2010 I deployed for six months to South America as part of a counter-narcotics operation. I was honestly dreading it, but I ended up loving the experience of being deployed. It was like being away at camp, but floating in the ocean and working non-stop. It was easy to distract myself while

I was out to sea, and keep my mind off of what I missed about home. I firmly believe that deployment is mentally harder on the service member's family than it is for the service member. We're out there floating and keeping one another entertained, while our families and loved ones are at home wondering how we're doing.

There's a lot I miss about that deployment. I miss the motion of the ship rocking me to sleep, and feeling the hum of the engine rattling my rack. I miss waking up to a new ocean sunrise every morning, while clutching a shitty cup of stale boat coffee. I miss standing in the smoke pit at night with the only light coming from my cigar's cherry and the glow of the Milky Way. I miss playing cornhole on the flight deck while the helicopter was flying, and having to account for the ship's movement when it was my turn to toss bags. I miss putting a big fat wad of Skoal in my lip from sun up to sun down. But what I miss the most is the guys. I really miss the guys.

I was lucky to deploy with a great group of guys. We all got along with one another. Everyone was well tempered, hilarious, and very professional. The most deep and interesting conversations I've had in my life, I had on that boat. The hardest I've ever laughed, was on that boat. Moments of joy, anger, sadness, and excitement were all collectively shared. It's a camaraderie that I had never felt before, or since, and I don't think I'll ever feel that level of camaraderie again. I miss everyone from that deployment; even the annoying ones.

Friendship isn't even the correct word to describe it. *Coworker* certainly is the wrong term to use. *Temporary family* is probably the closest analogy.

Our helicopter squadron was broken up by a dozen or so detachments, and each detachment was made up of maintenance personnel and pilots. Detachments would deploy when needed, and eventually my detachment was called up. We prepared for deployment, and got underway onboard a frigate.

Life on the boat was easy. Sure, the hours are long, but there's also a ton of downtime. When the helicopter wasn't flying, we'd conduct routine maintenance. When the helicopter was flying, we'd just sit around and shoot the shit. When our allotted flight hours were spent that month, we'd do required maintenance and then just hang out.

Life at sea was simple, but if I had kids at the time I think it would've been rough. Two of the guys in my detachment had kids born while we were out to sea. I remember it taking its toll on them. Tempers got short. Frustrations ramped up. It's understandable.

It's hard to explain what it's like floating on a ship for months at a time if you've never done it. I've often wondered if a lot of Naval aviators were selected to be astronauts because they're used to long stretches of isolation, repetition, and a general feeling of being stuck on a giant mechanical island. It makes sense to me.

My wife and I were awesome at deployment. Every chance I got, I emailed her. I'd call her on a pay phone in port whenever I could. I could only email her a few times a week, and sometimes we'd go a few weeks without being able to communicate. But we never once felt strained or distant. We really kicked ass at it.

At the time of the deployment, I had already planned on getting out of the military when I came home. By the time the deployment would be over, I'd only have two months left on my enlistment obligation. So, I think we both understood that deployment would just be a little speed bump in our relationship that we'd have to get through before planning the rest of our lives.

Now, whenever we hear couples talk about how they're going to miss one another over the weekend, we just roll our eyes. *Two days. Oh. Must be suuuuper hard.*

Like I said earlier, this deployment's objective was primarily counter-narcotics. I quickly became disenfranchised with the mission. I understand that the broad picture of the Navy's mission is presence of power, but the routine of searching fishing boats every day off the coast of South America felt ridiculous. And that's what we did. It was drug-runner wack-a-mole.

Multiple times a week we'd find a small boat, board that boat, and search their cargo. The search took hours; look through cargo under caught fish, and everywhere else it would be possible to hide narcotics. So much wasted time and energy.

In the six months we were deployed, we only found one stash. Let me repeat that. We floated in the ocean for six months, boarded boats nearly every day, and we only found one stash of cocaine. A helicopter detachment onboard a frigate full of sailors bobbed in the water for six months, boarding countless fishing vessels, sifting through their cargo, only to find one stash.

Like I said, I understand the broad picture of having a presence across the globe, but this mission just felt like we were pouring gasoline on tax dollars and tossing a lit match on top. We were all extremely busy in our day-to-day activities, and I personally felt fulfilled, but when I sat back and thought about what we were accomplishing, or rather not accomplishing, I started to get a little frustrated with the mission. I didn't get frustrated with the deployment or those above me in the chain of command; I just wondered what the hell we were doing out there.

Coming home from deployment was way weirder than leaving for deployment. That was the harder adjustment by far. I had a daily routine on the boat, and then all of a sudden I'm back to normal life. The folks I lived with for six months were gone. The world was no longer rocking back and forth. Oh! That reminds me. One of the strangest adjustments coming home was whenever I'd get in the shower, I felt like I was rocking. My body would physically sway back and forth as if I was at the mercy of the ocean's current. I never even considered that when I was coming home. I legitimately got sea sick in my shower because the world was stationary, and my body wanted the world to sway. Weird.

A few days after I was home, my mom gave me a call and told me that she had breast cancer.

That just tells you the kind of person she is. She didn't want to tell me while I was out to sea, and she didn't want to tell me as I was coming home. She wanted me to enjoy a few days at home before I heard the news, and she didn't want me to worry while I was away. Of course, at the time, I wish she would have told me. But I appreciate that decision in hindsight. The reason I wish she would have told me is because after being out to sea with my detachment, the guys became kind of a support system. Everyone helped everyone cope with life away. My shipmates had kids while they were gone, and we'd talk about it. Family members were sick, and we'd talk about it. It was truly a support system where everyone was literally in the same boat.

    I took the news of my mom's cancer hard. Luckily, thanks to modern medicine and an optimistic attitude like no other, everything worked out in the end. After two battles with breast cancer, she is now cancer free.

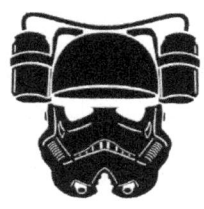

When I fulfilled my enlistment obligation and transitioned back to civilian life, I found myself reverting back to some of my old habits. I found that I lacked the motivation that I thought I'd have when I got out. I began to miss the structure and discipline. At first, I doubted my decision to leave. I quietly wondered to myself if I needed a regimented life in order to function. I later found out that a regimented life isn't necessarily one that comes from an external source; I could regiment myself.

My plan when I got out was to go to college using the Post-9/11 G.I. Bill. For those of you who don't know, the G.I. Bill is something all veterans have access to in order to pay for college. The government will pay for your schooling. It's an amazing deal. One that, if you're not able to pay for college out-of-pocket and don't want to sign on the dotted line for decades of student loan debt, can really give folks a fighting chance for their future.

Unfortunately, I procrastinated. I took a few classes a semester here and there, while working at a book store and as a graphic designer at a small company. I decided to slowly make my way through school, but looking back, I should have just knocked that shit out. But hey, you can't kick yourself in the ass for dumb decisions you made in the past. You can only learn from those dumb decisions and try to let them guide you a little bit. As of right now, I've been out of the Navy for seven years, and I only have about a year left until I earn my Bachelor's Degree.

I would never tell someone that they should join the military. It's not my decision to make, and oftentimes, I don't know the individual's situation. For me, it was a major turning point and one of the best decisions I've ever made. If you're struggling to find your place in the world, if you're directionless, if you think you need some discipline or guidance, if you want to learn a skill, see the world, or if you're just plain bored, I would highly recommend considering it an option.

One thing I think the Navy did for me was make me a less patient person, and that's something I'm trying to fix. When I was constantly on the go, being told where to go, what to do, how fast to do it, I believe that constant pressure to always be moving stuck with me. I don't like lollygagging. I have a hard time with indecisiveness. *Point yourself in a damn direction and move!* Like I said, I'm trying to correct this. I find that I'm often restless.

If I could do it all over again I might have decided to stick it out until retirement. At the time I'm writing this, I would only have eight years left until a twenty year retirement if I would have stayed in. There's just so much job security in it. To me, civilian life is way more wishy-washy and nerve-racking. Now that I'm a father, I think I made the right decision. I can't imagine being gone for year-long deployments and missing out on so much of my daughter's development.

I miss the Navy. I really miss it. I will always look back longingly at my time in the United States Navy. It was an adventure, a challenge, and an education like no other.

CHAPTER 7
VIDEO GAMES

One constant obsession I've had my entire life are video games. I primarily play multiplayer PC games, and have played with the same group of guys for over fifteen years. For me, playing a video game isn't just about exploring new worlds or reaching set goals; it's about staying in touch with my oldest friends. For the most part, everyone I play with, I also grew up with. The mischievous high school pranksters I mentioned earlier in the book are the same guys I play with multiple times a week.

There was once a stigma attached to people who play video games. You'd constantly hear, from dummies, that gamers were lazy and futureless. Video games were often touted as a waste of time and money. Are they? Obviously my opinion will come off as super biased, because I love playing games, but I don't think they're a waste of time or money at all. They are some of the cheapest sources of entertainment you can take part in.

Let's say you drop $60 on a brand new AAA title. $60 might sound like a lot of money, but in terms of bang for your buck, the entertainment value is hard to beat. Nowadays, the average leisurely completion time for many RPGs is over forty-hours. Over forty-hours of entertainment for $60? Can you find me another source of entertainment that is that long and that cheap? Hell, you'd have to watch roughly twenty movies to equal that length of time. The average movie ticket price in 2016 was $8.65.

$$20 \times \$8.65 = \$173.$$

Not including dinner, popcorn, and drinks.

My point is that video games, when compared to other forms of entertainment, are cheap. Don't get me wrong, I love going out. My weekends, before the baby, were often spent riding bikes with my wife to local breweries, and grabbing some delicious grub. But comparing dollar to value is how my dumb brain justifies dropping cash on video games. It makes sense to me.

Many games tell in-depth stories that rival the stories found in movies or television. They often present interesting and relatable characters that are memorable years after the credits roll. It can be argued that some of the best storytelling today is being written for video games. Sure, there's a lot shit mixed in, but that's no different than any other form of media. There are shitty movies, and there are shitty video games.

Let's take *Mass Effect* as an example. *Mass Effect's* lore is so extensive that, in time, it could possibly rival *Star Wars* in detail and scope. The characters are so fleshed out that they will be remembered as much as people remember their favorite sci-fi film heroes. The music is so cinematic that it often surpasses the emotional impact of music found in multi-million dollar blockbusters.

In the past, people questioned whether or not video games were art. Can you imagine anyone seriously posing that question today? I can't.

A video game can also be educational, even if its main goal isn't to teach. I have always enjoyed

World War Two video games, and while they have always been incredibly entertaining, they have also been unexpectedly educational. I credit my interest in the time period to *Call of Duty*, *Medal of Honor*, *WWII Online*, *Company of Heroes*, *Brothers in Arms*, *Day of Defeat*, and many other WWII era games. It may sound strange, but video games really did increase my fascination with World War Two, among other factors. I could learn about the machinery, the morality, and the sacrifice, all while having fun.

If it weren't for multiplayer games, I probably wouldn't be much of a gamer. I have a bad habit of starting single player games, playing them for a few hours, and then never touching them again. I don't know why. When I play a single player game, I sometimes feel like I'm disconnected from the world, and I need some human-to-human contact. Even if that contact is from strangers who are trying to hunt me down. A single player game has to really grab me in order for me to stick with it.

Off the top of my head, the last few single player games I finished were *Alien: Isolation*, *Assassin's Creed Syndicate*, *Bioshock Infinite*, *Max Payne 3*, and *Half Life 2*. That's a pretty damn short list for the past thirteen years. I'm sure I'm missing a few there, but they must've not been too memorable.

There's a feeling I can't really explain when I fire up a multiplayer game. It's a mixture of new experiences, the unexpected, and the variety of gameplay. Every match, no matter what game you're playing, is different than the last. Am I addicted to the variation? Am I addicted to that little shot of adrenaline I get when I see someone in *PlayerUnknown's Battlegrounds?* Maybe. Probably. Yeah, I am.

Like I said, if it weren't for multiplayer games, I probably wouldn't be much of a gamer. And if it weren't for the group of guys that I consistently play with, I probably wouldn't even play many multiplayer games. That's really what it's all about. The continued friendship, laughter, and just being able to keep in touch.

In the past, I think a lot of people had a misconception about gamers that they were all loners, isolated in their rooms, tapping away at buttons. I've been playing videos games, in one form or another, for nearly three decades, and that has never been the case. Games have always been an incredibly social experience. Arcades used to be the front line for thumb-warriors, but then the battlefield moved to the living room. Your home became the arcade. Not much longer after that, the digital combat zone became a global network. Now you could play with, or against, anyone on the planet.

So, if I had to choose between sitting down and watching a reality TV show for an hour, or playing a video game with folks from around the world, there's no contest. I'm going with the video game every time. At least with a video game I can interact with people, I can work on my hand-eye coordination, and I can take part in a compelling story. All of that sounds much more interesting to me than watching eleven seasons of *Duck Dynasty* or *The Real Housewives of Who Gives a Shit*.

I used to make maps for *Counter Strike: Source* and host my own server. I'd grab my sketchbook and draw an overhead view of what the map would look like, take that rough idea to Source SDK, and start modeling. I made a wild west saloon, a city block, a sewage system, and more. I really wish I had time to make my own maps again. The feeling of putting months of work into making a map, uploading it to your own server, and having random people play on it is amazing. I can't imagine how it must feel to design a game, or be a part of a development team. It must be such a rewarding experience to see your creations come to life.

The experience of designing my own maps really left an impression on me. Ever since then, I've wanted every multiplayer game to offer this capability. I can't think of a better way to keep your game alive and thriving than to allow the community to modify and create within your game.

Imagine a modern *Star Wars Battlefront* game that allowed you to host your own custom servers and easily design your own maps. What's frustrating about this not being the case, is that you could host, modify, and create in the original Battlefront games that were released in the mid-2000s. People still play those games because of that. Giving players the ability to be creative within your game ensures the longevity of your game. It gives a reason for people to continue to want to come back to your game. It allows communities to spring up within your game. And if there's one thing that will keep your game thriving for a long time, it's the community. Without community customization your game is doomed to experience a much faster death.

Maybe that's the goal of some of the huge publishers and developers; don't offer customization or modification so that the player is required to suck off the company's teat for any and all content. Make it so the player is required to buy DLC to continue playing. Don't allow players to make their own stuff, ensuring the game will die a faster death, and then you can release a sequel. It's not necessarily a bad thing; it's a great business model. But I look at games that have been going strong for decades, with big developer updates here and there, but truly thrive on community customization. Those games are the ones that I love. They're usually the ones that stick around.

I'm sure some of you guys remember how hyped I was when *Battlefront* (2015) was first announced. I kept saying how excited I was to host my own server and get the HelloGreedo community to play together. The idea of getting all of us playing together in one big server was more exciting to me than the idea of the game itself. I had enormous ambitions. I was willing to spend a good chunk of my own money to host a server, and turn HelloGreedo into a gaming community. I was extremely disappointed when I found out that there wasn't going to be a server browser and customization wasn't even remotely a thing.

The disappointed wasn't just because of the selfish desire to host a server, it was also the realization that the game wasn't going to last very long. It was the realization that cultivating a community wasn't necessarily in EA's playbook; at least in the way that I was hoping. It was a huge bummer, and still continues to be a bummer with *Star Wars Battlefront 2*.

When *Battlefront (2015)* was announced, I never imagined there wouldn't be a server browser in the game. I was, and still am, so accustomed to PC games that allow custom servers and modifications. The thought that those things weren't going to be in the game never crossed my mind. The idea of not including custom servers on the PC version of the game was like putting a car on the market with no back tires.

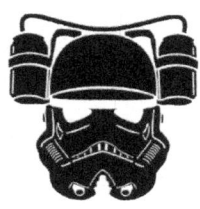

I don't hate microtransactions as much as most people it seems. I understand the concern they raise about gambling and addiction, but I also see how beneficial they can be for the longevity of a game and the success of a business.

Let me be clear; I've never once paid for a microtransaction in my life. I have zero desire to pay for a pistol skin in *Counter Strike* or a rare jacket in *PUBG*. I couldn't be more disinterested in a video game's feature than pointless cosmetics on a character that will only be seen for a split second by other players. The idea of people paying large sums of real world money for a rare crate that is basically a slot machine makes me a little angry.

I completely understand the desire to outfit your character in MMORPGs or even a game like *Destiny*, but I don't understand the point in a FPS. No one is going to see that super sweet dragon skin on your MP5. No one cares. Save your money.

Seeing the community outrage over EA's *pay to win* microtransaction system was actually pretty incredible. It was both an amazing thing to witness, and horrifying at the same time. It was amazing in that a vast majority of consumers stood up with one voice against a feature they were collectively against. It was terrifying for the exact same reason.

Look, we're not talking about healthcare or contaminated food. We're talking about a video game that you don't have to buy, don't have to play, and is under no obligation to cater to your every wish. I couldn't be a bigger consumer advocate, but being a consumer advocate, in my mind, means advocating for safety. Luke Skywalker being an unlockable character from the jump isn't something I have the energy to complain about.

I don't know what the future holds for *Star Wars Battlefront 2*, but I am extremely curious where the game would be right now if the original microtransaction system had stayed in place. The lack of vast non-cosmetic microtransaction revenue doesn't seem to have affected the free DLC that is being promised and pumped out. Ultimately, the steps that EA took to remove certain aspects of the microtransaction store was a good decision.

Community input is often a great way to gauge interest in certain features, but there's rarely a general consensus about what direction a project should go in. I often look at community input as being an extreme case of having too many cooks in the kitchen. When there are too many people involved in the management of something things often get muddied and ruined. You just need one conductor at the symphony. The audience doesn't stand there waving the stick.

I am an advocate for people and companies making what they want to make. As a consumer of art, I want it to be the purest form of what someone or an organization wants to make. The idea of an inexperienced mob dictating what direction a project goes in sounds like the most soulless pursuit I can imagine. When it comes to the consumption of art, and I consider video games art, I believe in absolute freedom without too much input from the digital horde or the suit and tie wearing executives.

Yes, I'm incredibly disappointed that there's no server browser in *Battlefront 2,* but my outlook and philosophy holds true. I'm sick of companies following trends in gaming, failing to innovate, and creating pockets of triple-A stagnation; but my outlook still holds true.

I don't get excited for these huge triple-A multi-million dollar titles like I used to. Most of them lack innovation, rehash the same ideas from previous installments, and cause me to shrug my shoulders with apathy. My excitement can be found in independent developers. That's where the true innovation is. Shoestring budgets and bright minds creating incredible games that push the boundaries of convention and take chances.

One of my favorite games in the past few years is called *The Swapper*. It's a puzzle-platformer developed and published by a small studio from Finland called Facepalm Games. *The Swapper* is challenging, charming, eerie, engaging, and insanely fun. Everything about the game is innovative and refreshing. The character you control has a cloning device that you use to navigate complex puzzles. It's hard to explain on paper. Look it up. I think you'll like it.

We truly are in the age of innovation, and it's not coming from the big studios, it's coming from the little guys. It's coming from a handful of people with passion and an idea. The abundance of independent games popping up left and right is without a doubt the most exciting thing in video games today. It's inspiring.

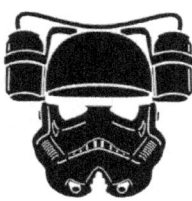

The first time I tried virtual reality (VR) was at my buddy's apartment. He just had a cheap VR headset that he bought from the convenience store, and that his smartphone snapped into. I didn't expect to be impressed by this cheap setup. I was wrong. My thoughts on the future of video games, entertainment, education, and reality in general changed that day.

I put the goggles on and sat down on the couch. A travel demo was loaded up and ready to go. I clicked play, and was instantly transported into another world. Sure, the resolution wasn't that great. Yeah, the full frame of my vision wasn't covered by the screen. But the most impressive thing was the head tracking. I couldn't get over how good this shitty headset tracked my motion.

The travel demo took me to different places on the globe, and eventually I found myself in Rome. The Colosseum was in the distance. I got closer and closer to it. I was looking around, keeping my vision relatively straight at shoulder height. I then looked down towards the ground, and saw a little girl holding her parent's hand. She was looking around, and suddenly looked up right at me. It was such a strange feeling. As if I was peering into another dimension. As if I was a ghostly entity floating in this other world. Obviously, she was just reacting to the camera that was there when they recorded the 360 degree footage, but my brain didn't see it that way. My eyes told my brain that I was looking at someone, who was looking at me, in a place that my body knew I wasn't in. It was a completely surreal experience.

I can't imagine where this technology will end up in the future. There's no doubt in my mind that in my daughter's lifetime there will be a VR experience indistinguishable from the real world. People will disappear into another existence. It will happen. The exponential growth of technology keeps on chugging along.

Practical uses of changing one's environment in digital space is also promising. Let's say you can only fit a tiny television in your tiny bedroom, but you want to watch the latest superhero movie on a screen the size of a movie theater screen. You can put on a pair of virtual reality goggles, and watch the movie in a digital movie theater. That blows my mind. You're technically watching the movie on a small screen only fractions of an inch away from your eyes, but the environment that you're looking at makes it *seem* like you're inside of a movie theater. So, you're watching the movie on an enormous screen inside of a tiny screen. I don't know why that blows my mind so much, but it does.

Obviously there are far more important possibilities with this technology than watching a movie in a fake theater. But it's neat to think about.

I've heard a lot of people speak fearfully about the future of virtual reality. I understand the concerns, but I'm not worried at all. Naysayers and cynics go hand in hand with every new world-changing piece of technology. There's always a group of people claiming the new gadget or gizmo will be the end of society as we know it.

One of the coolest experiences I've had because of the channel was becoming an EA Game Changer, and flying out to San Francisco in November of 2017 to play *Battlefront 2* before it was released. It was humbling. I didn't take it for granted at all. Truthfully, I couldn't wrap my brain around the fact that I had the opportunity. It's still hard for me to make sense of it all. Sure, I have this relatively large Star Wars YouTube channel. Yeah, I play the hell out of video games. I suppose I'm a good candidate for the program. But I still find it hard to believe that this silly channel I started in 2011 has allowed me to participate in some really neat stuff.

I hope I never lose that sense of wonder with all of this. I can see how constantly having these experiences would go to some people's heads. I can see how it would make some people jaded. I never want to feel entitled to any of it. I do not ever want to take any of it for granted. No one likes a cocky shithead who thinks they're owed something because they make silly internet videos. Stay humble. Stay grounded. Appreciate the opportunities.

That being said, it was an incredible experience. I'm looking forward to the next event I can attend when EA starts to feature new Star Wars games. Where are those new and different Star Wars games you may be asking yourself. Don't worry, I'm asking myself the same question.

When EA acquired the Star Wars license in 2013, I fully expected them to pump out game after game and milk the hell out of the franchise. I never expected to get two *Battlefront* games in six years; hopefully they have a lot being made right now, and hopefully they reveal what they're working on sooner rather than later. It definitely feels like we're in a Star Wars game drought. I'm crossing my fingers that that gets corrected soon.

My all-time favorite Star Wars game is *Star Wars Galaxies*. *Galaxies* was a MMORPG that released in 2003. The style of MMO that *Galaxies* was is the style of MMO that I've always gravitated towards.

In the game, you weren't just playing Star Wars; you were living in the Star Wars universe. You could take part in numerous non-combat professions, and live a life within Star Wars. Not everything was combat.

I was a doctor, owned a home, and lived in a guild city. I was never really into the combat of the game. Yeah, the combat was fun here and there, but I preferred using the game as my own personal sandbox and participating in the commerce. As a doctor, I could give people major stat buffs before they went out on a dangerous adventure. I would sit inside of the Mos Eisley spaceport and have a chat macro repeating that said something like *"NEED*

BUFFS? FULL BUFFS FOR 1,000 CREDITS. LINE UP. PAY FIRST. RECEIVE BUFFS". I'd sit there, have a line of fifty people patiently waiting in front of me, receive payment, and give buffs. I'm sure that sounds incredibly boring to some people, but for me it was some of the best times I've ever had in a video game. I was living in Star Wars. I was working in Star Wars. I was chatting in Star Wars. I was commuting in Star Wars. It was mind blowing.

I owned a home on Tatooine, and it was inside of a player-run guild city. Yep, guilds could have their own cities, and those cities could have spaceports, merchants, cantinas, and pretty much any other feature you'd find in NPC cities. If you wanted to, you could become the mayor of the city. There was actually a skill tree titled *politician*. The game was perfect for me in every way; things to do for those who just wanted to live inside of Star Wars, and not solely rely on combat to stay engaged.

In a way, *Star Wars Galaxies* feels like a relic; a game without levels, that did not hold your hand, and that allowed you to be anything you wanted to be. It was the antithesis of something like *World of Warcraft*, which is why when *Star Wars Galaxies* was later patched, turning the game into a *World of Warcraft* clone, an enormous percentage of the game's population left and never looked back. The game was an incredibly unique experience; one that I don't think we'll ever see again in a Star Wars game.

I could go on and on about my time playing *Star Wars Galaxies*. Whether how awesome it was that you couldn't just become a Jedi, you had to work for it. It could take a year; two years. You had to find the right things, do the right things; it was a puzzle that you and your character alone had to figure out. Or how you could furnish your home with trinkets you found around the galaxy. Or faction wars. I'll spare you the details. We'd be here for a while. But if you ever played the game, you know how truly special it was. When it comes to MMORPGs, *Star Wars Galaxies* and *Ultima Online* represent exactly what I look for in the genre.

CHAPTER 8
BEING A DAD

It still doesn't make sense, and it's impossible to put into words. The feeling of becoming a dad and watching your child slowly discover the world is indescribable. At the time I'm writing this, December 2018, my daughter is only eight months old. In those eight months she has gone from barely opening her eyes to babbling, rolling over, sitting up, smiling, laughing, sleeping through the night, napping on a regular schedule, and saying *"dada"*. She studies the world and people. She smiles when we smile. She pinches our faces. She waves when we wave. It's all mind-blowing.

When people ask me things like, "what's it like to be a dad?" My reply is usually along the lines of, *"oh it's amazing"* or *"it's a crazy feeling."* Those are both true statements, but what do they really mean? I don't know. Like I said, it's impossible to put into words. All the vocabulary and word-salad in the world can't even begin to contextualize the deep emotional sense that comes with being a parent. It is a love like no other.

The instant feeling I had when my daughter was born was how little my personal wants, needs, or desires mattered. As I told my wife, "I do not give a shit about myself anymore." My only goals in life now are to make my daughter happy, aid her natural curiosity, allow her to grow into her own person, and most importantly, have a fun childhood.

When my daughter was first born, she was laying on a little bed while the nurses made sure she was okay. She was crying as loud as humanly possible. For nine months, she was warm and cozy inside of her little pitch black biological home, and then, suddenly, she was pulled into a bright and loud world. She was once cocooned in her little safe, warm, and familiar world, and suddenly brought into the unknown. It must be terrifying. Obviously, we all went through it. None of us remember it. I never really thought about it until that day. What a drastic change.

My wife was in labor for a couple days. We went to the hospital three times, but they turned us back every time. She was in labor, but the doctors said it wasn't time; things weren't moving fast enough yet. So, we had a lot of false alarms. They didn't feel like false alarms, because my wife was in labor, and she was experiencing everything that goes along with that. As my dad has always said, if men had to give birth, there'd be no new people. I didn't fully understand what he meant by that until this experience.

I felt helpless, for a number of reasons. For one, I couldn't help my wife's pain. I tried to comfort her the best I could, but it was ultimately out of my control. Another reason I felt completely out of control was because I couldn't see my daughter. I knew she was in there, but I didn't know if she was okay. I knew I couldn't help her until she was out and present in the world. This little human that I already care so deeply about is behind an impossible wall, and I could do nothing if something was going wrong. I was scared shitless. I don't like the feeling of being out of control. I like being able to help and take action when at all possible. With no instruments to check on my daughter's condition in the womb, with no knowledge of how she was doing in there, I felt completely helpless. All the while, my wife was in excruciating pain, and I could do nothing to remedy the situation. It was a waiting game.

My nervousness and fear was amplified because of a miscarriage we had the year prior, which was by far the most heartbreaking experience of my life; one that I rarely talk about, but one that I think of quite often. It's an extremely common occurrence, as we later found out. Regardless, this time around, my brain was full of potentially devastating scenarios. Thankfully, it all worked out.

When the hospital eventually admitted us, we were rushed to a birthing room, where we would wait another twelve hours. The doctor administered a drug that is meant to induce labor, but that didn't help the process. Therefore, the doctor decided to move forward with a c-section. He was worried that something may have been wrong, and he wanted to act fast.

So, there I was, sitting outside of the operating room, waiting to be called in by the doctor. When I walked in, my wife was laying on the operating table with a curtain around her. I held her hand. We were both terrified. I reassured her that everything was going to be okay; I was also trying to convince myself the same. The doctor told me to peek over the curtain, and when I did, I saw our daughter's head; my first glimpse of our baby. When my daughter was pulled out, the nurses rushed her to a room to check her vitals and make sure everything was okay. I didn't hear a peep. No crying. No fussing. Nothing. For a brief moment, I thought the worst had happened. Within a minute, we began to hear the cries of our daughter from the next room. A tsunami of relief washed over me. The first hurdle had been overcome. I was about to meet my daughter for the first time.

My wife had to stay on the operating table. Undergoing a C-section is major surgery. The doctor and nurses had to make sure she was okay. So, they brought me to the room where my daughter was laying. She was crying as loud as humanly possible. She was pulled from her warm and comfortable home, and plopped on a cold and bright plastic bed. As I approached the bed, I began to cry. I looked at the two nurses and instinctually gave them both a big bear hug. My focus then turned towards my daughter.

She laid on her back, eyes closed; putting her lungs to work by screaming to the world that she had arrived. I bent down to her eye level, and began to say hello.

Through the chaos and noise, my seconds-old daughter's crying quickly stopped when she recognized my voice from months of being in the womb. Her terror seemed to turn to curiosity. She struggled to open her eyes for a peek. Despite the bright white lights, and nine months of darkness, she was able to open her eyes for a few seconds. This was the first time we saw one another. It was, and perhaps always will be, the most intense emotional experience of my life.

When I sat down to write this chapter, I had a hard time figuring out exactly what it would be. I knew that it would be difficult to put into words the feelings that I've been experiencing over the past eight months. It's proven to be even more difficult than I originally predicted. Like I said earlier, it's an indescribable feeling. One that words simply can't do justice.

When I open the door to my daughter's room in the morning, and her head pops up with a giant smile across her face, I melt. When she copies our hand movements, or our babbling noises, it's an amazing connection. When she observes the trees swaying in the breeze, or tilts her head towards the sounds of birds, all I want to do is nurture her innate curiosity and creativity. I look at all of this, at the age of eight months, and wonder what the future holds. I'm in no rush to get there, of course. She's already grown up so fast. These past few months have felt like a complete whirlwind. Despite that, her mom and I are so excited to start traditions, show her the world, encourage her to pursue what makes her happy, take her on fun family trips, and lead her down a path of self-discovery and adventure.

I think encouragement is fundamental. I've thought about this long and hard. In my own life, only until recently, I cared far too much about what people thought of me or what I was doing. I hope to instill in her a sense of independence and fearlessness. I hope to, among all else, be a force in her life that encourages her to find enjoyment in pursuits and paths she wishes to walk. I will never force her down paths; only urge her to chart her own course. I will never be an authoritarian figure. Rather, I hope to be someone she can come to for advice, but never pushy in demands. I hope to always recognize that her choices are her own, allow her to fail, dust herself off, and always be available for guidance if she seeks it. Above all else, I hope to be her friend.

Is all of that easier said than done? Of course. There's no question about that. We're still at the starting line; who knows where all of this will lead. I recognize that to work on raising a child, you also have to work on raising yourself in a way. You must try to improve yourself, in order to assist this new human who is trying to find their place in the world. I have never been more excited for a challenge in my entire life.

It's funny, I'm often asked the question *"what if she doesn't like Star Wars!?"* To which I reply, *"I don't give a shit."* My likes, loves, wants and wishes do not reflect what I want her to like, love, want or wish. I do not want to push her into liking what I like. Of course, my wife and I are going to share the things we like with her. But Star Wars? I don't care if she likes it or not. In the grand scheme of things, I'd rather her be interested in astronomy, camping, or science. Even those interests are things that I like; she doesn't have to like them.

There's something weird about pushing a kid to like the things you like. I don't know how to explain it. It's kind of like the football dad cliché. I have a friend whose dad pushed him into playing football, fervently, and he's resented it ever since. His dad loves football. He did not. It wasn't a give and take relationship, as far as he's told me. His father did not show interest in his son's interests. That's something I will never do. I will always show interest in my daughter's interests, nurture them, and help her learn more about them. Her interests will become my interests. If she's into dance, I'll be in the living room learning how to pirouette. If she's into painting, I'll buy some easels and we'll have family painting nights. If she's into some form of activism, I'll help her paint some signs and drive her to the picket line. No matter what her interests are, I'll show interest in them. Her autonomy makes me extremely excited for the future, and that growth to becoming an autonomous human being is something I'm excited to witness.

I often wonder what she'll be into, or what her voice will sound like, or what kind of person she'll grow up to be. There are so many things that I'm curious about that will eventually be revealed. I can't wait to see what the future holds. Once again, I'm in no rush. Seeing how fast these past eight months have gone certainly makes me pause and reflect.

When my wife and I walk into her room in the morning, the first thing I say is, "*It's a new day! It's a new day!*" That excitement for life, for the start of a new day, for the possibilities of what the next moment holds, is something I hope to instill in her above all else.

One of the things that blows my mind whenever I think about it is the fact that everything is new to her. Literally everything that she sees, hears, tastes or smells is a new discovery. She is exploring a new world. The smallest things that we take for granted, she is fascinated by. Mirrors are a major example of this. We'll sit in front of the mirror, she'll look at the mirror and then look at me with a big smile on her face. She'll reach out, hesitate to touch the mirror, and then look at me to see what my reaction is. Her fascination and curiosity makes me fascinated! I wonder what she's thinking. When she looks at herself in the mirror, and slowly recognizes that the image she's looking at is herself, I can't help but be amazed.

Or when we put on music, we can literally see how her enjoyment of different songs or genres changes. She loves Motown by the way. When *Something's Got A Hold On Me* by Etta James comes on, she starts kicking with excitement and gets a huge smile on her face. It's too damn cute.

One of the things I'm most excited to do as a family is go camping. We have a six-person tent that perfectly fits an air mattress. Florida Caverns State Park is a place my wife and I have camped at before, and it's a spot we definitely want to take our daughter to. Dark and damp caves filled with various rock formations, surrounded by clear springs. For whatever reason, the thought of taking our daughter on these types of trips gets me extremely excited; a little break from the technological day-to-day. A little weekend adventure to learn and explore.

It's funny, when she goes down for a nap or we lay her in the crib for the night, I miss her. I know she's just one room over and I'll see her in a few hours, but I miss her. That smile and playful spirit instantly eases all my worries. It's infectious!

The world, to her, is a new place to explore. It's full of scary things, funny things, and things to investigate and learn. It's our job as parents to always be there to help guide her through this weird and whacky world the best we can. After all, we are her safety blanket. We are all she knows. We are her protectors and helpers. She looks at us to be there for her. When we aren't around, she's looking for us. It's a big responsibility, and one that should not be taken lightly.

In the grand biological game of chance, we have been connected. Out of all the possibilities that could have been, and the possibilities that never will be, we have been put together. The billions of years, stars forming and dying, countless generations born and surviving, the luck of things lining up perfectly for her to be here with us in this small instant on the cosmic calendar; it's a connection like no other.

I hope my daughter gets more of my wife's traits than mine. I fly by the seat of my pants and rarely plan anything. I have a very lackadaisical attitude about most things, and rarely deem anything to be a big deal. My wife on the other hand loves to plan, often sees situations more serious than I do, and is future oriented. I tend to live in the now to a fault, and she often wants to plot a course for what's to come. Obviously, a mix of the two would be great, but if she gets a little more of one of us, I really hope it's her mom!

My wife has been amazing through all of this. I don't tell her that nearly as much as I should. From carrying the baby, to her labor, to being a mother, I couldn't have hoped for anything more. Again, she's a planner, and I'm forgetful. She researches what we need to do, and we do it. If it weren't for her, I would be in big trouble. I wouldn't know what the hell to do.

Seeing my wife and my daughter play is amazing, and it must be even more amazing for my wife. She carried her for nine months, and then all of a sudden the baby that you've been taking care of inside you is sitting right in front of you. I talk about how deep my connection is with my daughter, but it must pale in comparison to my wife's, just on those facts alone.

I took a picture of my wife the first time she held our daughter. Out of all the pictures I've ever taken, I think it's my favorite. A mother and a daughter meeting for the first time; there's no words to describe it.

I don't know what the future holds. I don't even know what to hope for. All I aim to do is be the best dad I can be; helpful, encouraging, engaging, and her friend.

In 2017 my wife and I took a nine day road trip out west in a rented RV. We drove 1,452 miles, camped at six national parks, and visited three states. Out of all the fun trips we've ever been on, that is the one I'm most excited to share with my daughter. I want to share that experience with her. I want to hike miles of trails and stay up late gazing up at the Milky Way. I want to roast s'mores over the campfire and rock out to Bob Seger on the drive. I want to show my daughter the world.

One of things I'm most excited to witness is my wife and my daughter's relationship. I can just picture them going out and doing things together, chitchatting on the floor while eating a big bowl of ice cream, gossiping, watching movies, and just being one another's best friends. I've never understood parents that have a bad relationship with their kids.

Whenever I've come across those examples, I've found that it's often the parents who are either too controlling and don't let their kids become their own person. That will definitely not be the case. My wife is such an awesome role model for my daughter. We're both lucky to have her!

I want to encourage my daughter to go on trips with her friends, and explore all she can. I've had an amazing core group of friends for twenty years. We all keep in touch. We've all been in one another's weddings. Every year since we were sixteen, we've gone on big road trips. After all these years, we still rent a cabin together in the North Georgia mountains, catch up, go whitewater rafting, and hang out. Those trips are some of my favorite memories, and I want my daughter to have amazing memories with her friends too. It's important.

I don't know what else to say in this chapter. Becoming a dad has been such a huge life-changing event; one that I wouldn't trade for anything in the world. The future is brighter because of my daughter. My plans and goals are more attainable because of my daughter. Trips will be more fun because of my daughter. Going to the movies will be more enjoyable because of my daughter. Playing video games will be more fun with my daughter by my side. Everything is better since I've become a dad.

CHAPTER 9
SUPPORTER Q&A

The following questions come from channel sponsors and patrons; members of **The Fleet**. These are viewers who have chosen to support the channel on a monthly basis. I am forever grateful for their words of encouragement, patience, and support.

It is an absolute fact that the channel would not survive without their support and those who support my live streams. On top of that, I am beyond grateful for this support because it has allowed me to work from home and take care of my daughter. Support from **The Fleet** has given me the freedom to make YouTube videos, take the occasional freelance gig when necessary, and be a work-at-home dad.

Thank you, shipmates.

"How do you plan on improving your YouTube channel in the future?" – Antonio Belvees

I rarely, if ever, make plans for the channel. The most planning I do is usually on a week to week basis. I'll have a little notebook on my desk and jot down some simple ideas for videos I want to make during the week. That being said, I would like to be a little more active during big periods in the world of Star Wars; movie releases, book releases, game releases, etc.

I've found that a lot of times I have grand plans to make a ton of videos surrounding the premiere of a film, and I drastically underperform in what I was hoping to accomplish. Being topical on YouTube is paramount. The success of a Star Wars YouTube channel, at least from what I've experienced, has a lot to do with the amount of official Star Wars content coming out. When a film is getting close to its release date, the channel receives a significant bump in attention. I have often felt like I failed to capture that attention to my full ability. I don't know why, but when I see a lot of people covering a similar topic, I often shy away from said topic. It almost seems unintentional; just something in my brain thinks *all of these people are talking about this thing, what's the point of me talking about it too?* That is definitely a silly thought to have; people seem to want to know my opinion of whatever is coming down the pike.

So, to answer your question, my only plans are to be more proactive around movie release dates and try to capture the attention of people searching for Star Wars content. Other than that, I'll continue to fly by the seat of my pants!

"Having a newborn can sometimes make you ponder in the early hours of the morning about your own mortality - will I be around long enough to see them grow, achieve life goals, become a grandfather etc. Now you have a wonderful daughter has your perspective changed on your own mortality?" – *Tony Zotti*

When I look at my daughter, a sense of time certainly comes into play. She is eight months old at the time I'm typing this, and it feels like she was born yesterday. We all know that time flies, and it seems to get faster the older you get, but I don't think I grasped it fully until she was born.

I begin to think about the biological path that had to go perfect for billions of years for us to be here in this moment; ancestors struggling to survive, children born, people dying, migrating around the globe, and marching on without modern conveniences. It's incredible to think of history's path plotting its course to the present moment. I then think about future generations that will continue our path, and keep the biological train moving forward. We are all ancestors to the future, and that thought certainly makes me pause and ponder my own mortality.

I'd be lying if I said I never thought about what her life would be like if some tragic and unforeseen event happened to my wife or me. A lot of people grew up not knowing their biological parents, and that is gut-wrenching to me; both for the child and for the parent. As a parent, you want to always be there for your kids. You want to see them grow into adulthood, protect them, guide them, watch them explore the world, fall in and out of love, make memories, start traditions, and become parents themselves. The idea of that being taken away from a parent is heartbreaking. Much of life is out of our control. Destructive events surrounding us on a day-to-day basis have a way of sneaking up and surprising us. I suppose all you can do is take care of yourself, play the game as safe as possible, and keep your head on a swivel. Other than that, it's best to just accept the waves and ride them. My only goal, my only mission in this existence, is to see my daughter through her life until I am no longer a necessity. I accept and embrace the fact that I have an expiration date; I do not accept the fact that she has one as well.

"You can have one Jedi power ... but only one ... which one would have been the most useful in your life?" – *Paul Robinson*

The Jedi mind trick would probably be most useful in regular life, right? Of course it would be completely unethical. Imagine just walking around on a day to day basis; *you WILL give me all the money in the world.* That is a power no one should have, not even a Jedi! What's funny is that the mind trick is one of those powers that would realistically be used non-stop. Anyone with the ability would be getting their way left and right. Of course that wouldn't make for fun storytelling. The Force, and the powers that come from wielding it, often create plot holes. *Why didn't he use super-duper jump!? Why didn't he use the Jedi mind trick!? Why didn't he just levitate that thing!? Why isn't everyone a Force ghost!?* And then rationalizations for why the characters didn't do those things have to be applied. I'm off track.

While the mind trick would be the most useful, it's certainly not ethical, and I wouldn't want that power. I'd want something way more innocuous. I'd probably go with Force jump or something like that. I'd be the most out of shape, world class high-jumper in the NBA. I'd subtly use it. Maybe just jump a foot higher than everyone else; keep it relatively believable.

Or maybe I'd go with the Jedi mind probe; the ability to read minds. I'd become the longest running Jeopardy contestant in history. The question would come up; I'd pop into Alex Trebek's mind, see the answer, and buzz in.

Most Jedi powers wouldn't be that useful in regular life. Sure, you'd be able to leap on top of your roof to check for a leak. Yeah, you'd be able to bring the TV remote towards you if it was on the other side of the room. But a lot of them would just be way too powerful and intrusive for me to want.

> **"If you could go back in time and change one event in human history, would you? And if so, what would you change?"** – *Harry Reed*

I don't think I'd want to change a single thing. Changing one thing, no matter how horrible, would inadvertently change everything that came after it. Major cultural steps may not happen. The coming together and cooperation of nations might not have blossomed. We learn from the past. History is a wonderful guide; we record it in order to guard against perpetuating destructive patterns, and so that we can be inspired to greatness by history's greats.

I hope a time machine never gets invented. Well, I take that back. I'd love to see the future. I don't have much desire to see or visit the past. To me, seeing the future would be way more interesting. We have a general idea of how people lived in the past; what they did, systems of governance, wars, oppression, famine, you name it. I'm happy with that knowledge. Obviously there are a lot of unknowns, and a lot is missing from the historical record, but the future is where I would want to dial my DeLorean.

We only have a short amount of time on this planet, and I would love to be able to peer into the mystery of the future and see how humanity makes out. I'd love to be able to see how far we're able to push the boundaries of space exploration and technology. I'd love to see what this planet full of crazy primates is able to accomplish.

> **"How has putting on the helmet (or in other words choosing to be anonymous online) changed you or added to the channel? Would it be different if we knew your name and your face?"** – *MothMeta*

That's an interesting question. Honestly, I'm getting pretty damn sick of the helmet. It adds a lot more work to the video making process. Instead of just turning on my camera and talking, I have to record audio separate, edit the audio, put on my helmet, play the audio over my speakers, mime in front of the camera, and then mesh it all together in post. It would be so much easier if I could just turn on the camera and go.

That's not the only reason I'm getting sick of the helmet though. I feel like it's held me back from doing some cool shit in the past; panels and events. Because of some mystery that I wanted to keep up, I've opted out of a bunch of opportunities. I'm trying to correct that, though.

The helmet gimmick has been a ton of fun, don't get me wrong. I've never let it impede my creativity; whatever I say on the channel while wearing a helmet, I would say on the channel without wearing the helmet. In other words, it hasn't been used as a shield to hide myself in order to mount relentless anonymous attacks. I have tried, successfully in my opinion, to use the anonymity for fun, rather than as some protective layer to spew bullshit without repercussion.

I enjoy writing skits with the helmet in mind. For whatever reason, the idea of Stormtroopers doing normal every day stuff is funny to me. So, whenever I write a skit that involves Stormtroopers doing mundane stuff, I get a kick out of it. The downside to that is facial expressions. Sometimes I'll have an idea for a skit and realize that the joke would play way better if I was able to show some facial expression. There are definitely positives and negatives to wearing the bucket. Overall, I think it's been pretty positive. It's a fun gimmick, and gives the channel a unique identity.

"What were your initial thoughts when your first video blew up?" – *Clayton Boler*

When I decided to start the channel, I wanted to come out of the gate with a bang. I didn't want to make an introduction video or anything like that. *"Hi. I'm HelloGreedo I will be making Star Wars videos on this channel".* I wanted my first video to represent what the channel was going to be, rather than *telling* people what the channel was going to be.

So, when my first video started to gain traction, it was pretty damn exciting. My only thought was, *I want to make more videos.*

There was no money in it back in those days. The channel wasn't monetized, and to this day I've never seen a single penny from any of my *changes* videos. I just wanted to make a thing and was happy that people wanted to watch the thing I made. At that time, I saw the channel as nothing more than a project of passion.

I still remember the feeling of getting my first one-hundred subscribers. It was mind blowing that one-hundred people wanted to watch and listen to the dumb stuff I was making.

My first video didn't really start taking off until it was announced that Disney bought Star Wars, and that they were making episode 7. That's when the channel really started to blow up, understandably. Star Wars was back in the minds of millions, and topical videos always seem to do well.

So, my initial thought was that I just wanted to make more videos. That's really it. The process of creating something is way more rewarding, in my opinion, than uploading it or even having it seen by millions of people. There's something magical about having a blank screen just waiting for you to fill it up with whatever you want. I still feel that magic to this day. I love jumping into a project that will take me days, weeks, or even months to finish. The process of creation is one that I will never grow tired of.

"Do you feel that being an influencer on the YouTube platform has been integral to your own personal growth?" -
AT-AT Chat

Absolutely. There's no question about it. For one, being able to communicate with people from all around the world, hear different opinions, and better understand why people love what they love has been incredibly rewarding and educational. It's made me less combative, and more understanding. That is a byproduct of the channel that I could have never predicted.

Another byproduct of the channel has been aiding my communication skills, which I accredit to live streaming. Live streaming has been a really great way to practice thinking on my feet and formulating thoughts as fast as possible.

More than anything though, I think it's taught me that I can manage myself and my time better than I ever expected. It's shown me that if I have a passion for something and enjoy something, the hours of *work* I put into it never gets old or feels stale. The feeling I get when a dumb idea for a video pops in my head is invigorating, and actually creating it is incredibly rewarding. For a long time I wondered if I needed the Navy's structure, discipline, and regiment in order to stay focused. I've learned that that is not the case. HelloGreedo has been a very introspective process; one that has taught me a lot about my work ethic and drive.

That being said, there are days that I just don't feel like doing shit. There are plenty of those days. Sometimes I feel like a story has been beaten to death and giving my opinion on it would just be white noise. Sometimes I just don't have the motivation to work on a project. Those days are much rarer than the days that I feel the urge to work on stuff. I guess in that way, it's a lot like any other project, job, or task. Sometimes you're into it, sometimes you're not. Whenever I feel like that, I just let my attitude in the moment guide me, because if I forced myself to make something when I wasn't feeling it, the entire process would start feeling like a drag.

"What was your favorite memory from the time in the Navy?"
– Ryan Harp

My favorite memories from my time in the Navy all come from deployment. When you're not deployed, being in the Navy feels like any other job. But on deployment, it's kind of like being at summer camp with a bunch of dudes who all have the same disgusting sense of humor, never get upset about jokes, horse around, play games, smoke cigars, and hang out during downtime.

Some of my favorite memories are pulling into port, getting off the boat with a few of my friends, and exploring the local places. We were in Panama a lot and walked through tiny towns in Guatemala; grabbing beers at random bars or restaurants, and trying to find some Wi-Fi that actually worked so we could contact home.

Even when we were on the ship and working all day, it wasn't bad at all. We'd make stupid videos, wrestle in the aviation berthing (which sometimes got a little too aggressive), and put lawn chairs on the flight deck at night while we enjoyed some Cuban cigars we bought in port. I'm sure if I deployed with a different crew it'd be a different story, but everyone that I deployed with was awesome. I got really lucky with that.

My buddy from Puerto Rico brought his Xbox 360, and sometimes we'd hook it up to an old TV in the hangar and play *Call of Duty* at night. I'm definitely making it sound like more of a vacation than it actually was, trust me. It was fun regardless, and I'm honestly kind of bummed that I'll never experience it again.

Anyway, I don't have single favorite memory of my enlistment; it's more of a culmination of memories that make up the entire experience. Truthfully, the best memory might be coming home. My girlfriend, now wife, stood with my family and held a big welcome home sign. It felt damn good to be home.

CHAPTER 10
IN CLOSING

I don't even remember what the hell I talked about in this book. Holy hell, I never imagined it would be nearly as long as it is. If you're reading this sentence, that means you've finished *Sorry About the Mess.* Take a picture of this paragraph and shoot me a Tweet! Congratulations (*and sorry*), you made it through a bit of my mind!

I started writing this book, unintentionally, in April of 2016 between two college classes. I purposefully enrolled in two classes with a four hour break in between because I wanted to give myself a window to write videos. I didn't live close enough to the campus to justify driving home, so I saw it as a perfect opportunity to knock out stuff for the channel.

While I did write videos during those four hours, I also started writing down random thoughts. I ended up categorizing and organizing those random thoughts into (semi) cohesive chapters. It was a happy accident.

When I decided to actually turn this into a book, I didn't expect anyone to want to read it, and I still don't. Why? I don't know. I guess in my own dumb brain the idea of people wanting to read a bunch of messy nonsense that I wrote down will always be a foreign concept to me. As you all know, I tend to be quite self-deprecating. The idea of this mask-wearing nobody on the internet who talks about Star Wars putting out a book was kind of silly. It is silly. Who am I? Why do I think I can write a book? That's just those George McFly thoughts creeping back in. Eventually, I said to hell with it! Even if no one reads it or no one likes it, I'll be proud of the accomplishment.

A lot has changed in my life since I started this thing in 2016; mainly becoming a dad. If I could go back and rewrite the chapters, my thoughts on certain subjects might be different than what is represented here. As I've gone back to read through the book, I've wanted to change entire sections, but I've resisted the temptation. I cringe at some of the things I've written and the way I've written them, but that's part of the fun. This is kind of a time capsule, and just like everything you create, it represents your thoughts at the time. I'm sure in ten years when I sit down with a big cup of coffee to read *Sorry About the Mess*, I'll cringe, I'll laugh, and I'll be proud that I saw this project through to the end.

So, what's next? Well, around the same time that I started writing this book, I also started writing a science-fiction book. I only have about twenty pages written so far, and I haven't added to it in over a year, but I might make that my next long-term project. I think something like that; creating a story out of thin air, molding characters, structuring a narrative, and putting out a fictional story would be incredibly rewarding. Like this book, I have no delusions that anyone would want to read it. But I have a firm belief that if one's main goal is outside approval, acceptance, or attention, then the object of creation will suffer and nothing will ever get done. So, I'll write for myself, and maybe a few folks will dig it.

Other than that, I'll just keep doing what I'm

doing. It's work out okay so far.

With all of that being said, I just want to say thank you for reading these sloppy pages. Thank you for supporting the channel. Thank you for being a part of HelloGreedo. Thank you for tuning in. Thank you for caring. Thank you for being level headed. Thank you for coming on this journey with me. Thank you for everything. Without you, the channel would be lifeless. It's been fun.

HelloGreedo, out.

Made in United States
North Haven, CT
27 November 2022